To Lift a Mirror, for What You've Lost

MY LIFE IN AFGHANISTAN AND THE UNITED STATES

NANGY GHAFARSHAD

I0026598

F⊕RTIS

A NON-FICTION IMPRINT FROM ADDUCENT

Adducent, Inc.

www.Adducent.co

Titles Distributed In
North America
United Kingdom
Western Europe
South America
Australia

To Lift a Mirror, for What You've Lost

MY LIFE IN AFGHANISTAN AND THE UNITED STATES

Nangy Ghafarshad

Copyright © 2012 All rights reserved. No part of this book may be reproduced or transmitted in any form or by any means, electronic or mechanical, including photocopying, recording or by any information storage and retrieval system, without written permission from the publisher, except for brief quotations as would be used in a review.

Hardcover ISBN: 978-1-937592-10-3
Paperback ISBN: 978-1-937592-14-1

Published by Adducent, Inc. under its Fortis non-fiction imprint

Jacksonville, Florida

www.Adducent.co (*that's right, it's not a .com*)

Published in the United States of America

All statements of fact, opinion, or analysis expressed are those of the author and do not reflect the official positions or views of the publisher. Nothing in the contents should be construed as asserting or implying authentication of information or endorsement of the author's views. This book and subjects discussed herein are designed to provide the author's opinion about the subject matter covered and is for informational purposes only. Wikipedia was the source used for all historical and current information used on the regions covered in this book.

About the Author

Fifty-two years ago, Nangy Ghafarshad first arrived in the United States. A graduate of the Afghanistan military academy and an officer in the Royal Afghan Air Force in 1960 he reported for additional training with the United States Air Force. A fully rated fighter pilot, he was sent to the Soviet Union in 1965 to train in MiG-21 advanced fighter aircraft and was a member of the Afghan Air Force flight aerobatics team. In 1968 he returned to the U.S. to attend a United States Air Force sponsored leadership program. At the completion of that program, struggling with strong feelings of dismay at how his government ruled his native land and not wishing to return to a place offering little opportunity, he chose to resign his commission in the Royal Afghan Air Force and stay in Southern California, ultimately becoming a U.S. citizen.

While working as a corporate pilot (including flying Mrs. Rosalind Carter around California when Mr. Jimmy Carter ran for president) and as a flight instructor, in 1973 Nangy and his wife Fahima bought a small coffee shop in Claremont, California. Only 40 seats at the time, it has grown to a first-class restaurant that can seat 400 guests. Walter's Restaurant is now widely known and one of the finest dining experiences in Southern California. Nangy and Fahima are active in the following charitable organizations and efforts: international orphan care, an Afghan children's fund, Project Sister and House of Ruth.

For a span of 13 months (2009/2010) Nangy served as a Senior Cultural Advisor in Afghanistan to the U.S. Department of Defense. It was an opportunity to go back to the country of his birth to do something positive. That experience, in part, is the reason for this book.

Dedication

I dedicate this book to my wife, Fahima, who was with me and a constant support throughout my journey in life. My dreams wouldn't have come true without her love and support.

I also dedicate this book to my daughter Asya and her husband, Kurt, my son, Dawoud, his wife, Laila and my grandchildren Shaheen, Massoud, Mateen, and Farrah. They are the love of my life.

Acknowledgments

I have lived and learned in the United States for more than forty years, but I still think, dream and construct my sentences in Dari (my native language) and English. This book would have been a combination of both languages without help from my friend Dennis Lowery, and his team, who patiently read and reorganized my thoughts.

I also thank my dear friend, Baray Karim, who listened and motivated me to write this book during our walks at midnight in camp Marmal, Mazr-e-Sharif, Afghanistan.

My dear friend (by Rumi)

Translated by Nader Khalili

My dear friend
never lose hope
when the beloved
sends you away.

If you're abandoned
if you're left hopeless
tomorrow for sure
you'll be called again.

If the door is shut
right in your face
keep waiting with patience
don't leave right away.

Seeing your patience
your love will soon
summon you with grace
raise you like a champion.

And if all the roads
end up in dead ends
you'll be shown the secret paths
no one will comprehend.

The beloved I know
will give with no qualms
to a puny ant
the kingdom of Solomon.

My heart has journeyed
many times around the world
but has never found
and will never find
such a beloved again.

ah I better keep silence
I know this endless love
will surely arrive
for you and you and you.

Table of Contents

FOREWORD

The Story of My Life (by Rumi)
Translated by Nader Khalili

I was ready to tell
the story of my life
but the ripple of tears
and the agony of my heart
wouldn't let me

I began to stutter
saying a word here and there
and all along I felt
as tender as a crystal
ready to be shattered

in this stormy sea
we call life
all the big ships
come apart
board by board

how can I survive
riding a lonely
little boat
with no oars
and no arms

my boat did finally break
by the waves
and I broke free
as I tied myself
to a single board

though the panic is gone
I am now offended
why should I be so helpless
rising with one wave
and falling with the next

I don't know
if I am
nonexistence
while I exist
but I know for sure
when I am
I am not
but
when I am not
then I am

now how can I be
a skeptic
about the
resurrection and
coming to life again

since in this world
I have many times
like my own imagination
died and
been born again

that is why
after a long agonizing life
as a hunter
I finally let go and got
hunted down and became free

When we entered Afghanistan airspace the view of the mountainous terrain full of snow reminded me of when I flew over them as a Royal Afghan Air Force pilot.

Where I live in the United States, I am close to a mountain range where it snows during the winter, but these mountains, of my native land, are very different. Seeing them took me back to another time in my life. It reminded me of the people who live around these mountains in the most primitive way of life but their roots are so deep and structured by tradition that they are perversely proud that the most powerful nation of the world, the United States, has difficulty understanding why they behave the way they do.

We landed at Kabul International Airport. Things looked very different from what I remembered from forty years before. Many types of helicopters and airplanes (from different countries) were parked one after another. A few torn or blown up airplanes were nearby as well. It did not look like the same country I left so long ago. I remembered the main H.Q. of the Afghan Air Force was next to the Kabul airport. At that time the terminal itself, though small and third world, had charm, a relatively good restaurant and people came wearing their nicest outfits to greet passengers. Now I didn't see the terminal, or the restaurant. Everything was filthy and broken.

My wife, Fahima, and I couldn't hold back our tears. Through them we saw our country, which besides being primitive, was now ruined. The innocence of the country that I knew was gone. When we got out of the airplane, my cousin Mary (Mauree Jan Ashraf) was waiting for us with a car. She warned me not to hug and hold her like we used to. Unlike the way she dressed while in the west, she was now covered from head to toe.

The road to Kabul was totally different; many traffic circles and shack-like stores all around the street. Most buildings had barbed wire surrounding them for safety. One traffic circle, named after the war hero Ahmad Shah Massoud (who fought the Soviets during their invasion and occupation of Afghanistan), was the most dangerous where suicide bombers (a tactic from Iraq) got close to a car they suspected was carrying foreigners then blew up themselves and the cars around them. Check points by coalition and Afghan security forces were all around us.

We headed toward the house where my cousin lived, which was next to the palace. I remembered the palace and the streets around it but I couldn't tell where I was. Most of the roads were barricaded and unrecognizable, barbed wire and guards were everywhere. On the streets were hundreds and hundreds of taxis. When we were last in Kabul there were just a few cars.

We went to famous Chicken Street (where you could find the freshest fruits and foreign canned foods). It was not the same. This street was not very far from the house where I grew up. I told the driver to take us there, but to my disappointment I couldn't find my old home. The roads were barricaded and when we got out of the car there were beautiful kids begging everywhere. As we passed by every corner, the flashback of my youth, my friends, our playgrounds; nothing matched—nothing I saw was the same.

Fahima, and I cried for days.

I think it was at that point, even if only subconsciously at the time, when I knew I must write this story.

It's largely about me and my family; where we came from, some of our past and present—and some about the future. Throughout it you'll find a message of faith and belief in one's self and in following your heart. And it's about doorways that we step through in life. It's been said, "When one door closes, another one opens." I believe this to be true—it has been so for me personally.

It is sad that for Afghanistan those doors continue to lead to tenuous structures often without walls and ceilings; no roof, no stability. Just an opening that exposes its people to any number of outside influences and interference. To understand more of how that is so, in this story, I've included some of Afghanistan's past, present and thoughts on its future as well.

Perhaps what follows in my story will only be of interest to my family but for other readers I promise that there are things you will glean from the reading and that you will learn about Afghanistan that you did not know before. I hope that you will sit for a while, read my story and even listen to the words and what they share with you.

—Nangy Ghafarshad, Claremont, California
April 2012

INTRODUCTION

Birdwings (by Rumi)
Translated by Coleman Barks

Your grief for what you've lost lifts a mirror
up to where you're bravely working.
Expecting the worst, you look, and instead,
here's the joyful face you've been wanting to see.
Your hand opens and closes and opens and closes.
If it were always a fist or always stretched open,
you would be paralyzed.
Your deepest presence is in every small contracting and
expanding,
the two as beautifully balanced and coordinated
as birdwings.

**To understand Afghanistan and its people requires you know
something of its history.**

Many things have been stolen from the Afghan people over the
centuries. The least of which was a fabulous diamond. In the legend
that surrounds it, one of Nader Shah's (Nader Shah Afshar, King of
Persia) consorts supposedly said, *"If a strong man should take five
stones, and throw one north, one south, one east, and one west, and
the last straight up into the air, and the space between filled with gold
and gems, that would equal the value of the Koh-i-Noor."*

The beginning of modern Afghanistan can be dated to 1747, when the
Afghans in Nadir Shah's, army returned home after the king was
assassinated. Their leader, Ahmad Shah Abdali, who was only 25 years
old, protected the harem of the king from his enemies and was

rewarded with the Koh-i-Noor diamond. The origin of the diamond is unclear. Some sources believe the Koh-i-Noor was found more than 5,000 years ago, and is mentioned in ancient Sanskrit writings under the name Syamantaka.

In 1830, Shah Shuja, the deposed ruler of Afghanistan, managed to flee with the Koh-i-Noor to Lahore where it was given to the Sikh Maharaja (King) of Punjab, Ranjit Singh; in return for this Maharaja Ranjit Singh won back the Afghan throne for Shah Shuja-ul-Mulk.

Maharaja Ranjit Singh was crowned ruler of Punjab and willed the Koh-i-Noor to the Jagannath Temple in Orissa from his deathbed in 1839. But after his death the British administrators failed to execute his will. On 29 March 1849, the British raised their flag on the citadel of Lahore and the Punjab was formally proclaimed to be part of the British Empire in India. One of the terms of the Treaty of Lahore, the legal agreement formalizing this occupation, was as follows:

> The gem called the Koh-i-Noor which was taken from Shah Shuja-ul-Mulk by Maharajah Ranjit Singh shall be surrendered by the Maharajah of Lahore to the Queen of England.

It is believed that the Koh-i-Noor carries with it a curse and only when in the possession of a woman will the curse not work. All the men who owned it have either lost their throne or had other misfortunes befall them. Queen Victoria is the only reigning monarch to have worn the gem. According to the legend, if the monarch is a male, the stone is passed to his spouse.

The possibility of a curse that comes with ownership of the diamond dates back to a Hindu text relating to the first authenticated appearance of the diamond in 1306: "*He who owns this diamond will own the world, but will also know all its misfortunes. Only God, or a woman, can wear it with impunity.*"

All the owners of the Koh-i-Noor have had a tragedy befall them.

India has claimed the diamond and that the Koh-i-Noor was stolen from them and should be given back. When Elizabeth II made a state visit to India marking the 50th anniversary of Independence in 1997, many in India and Britain, including several Indian MPs, demanded the return of the diamond. In a July 2010 interview, British Prime Minister, David Cameron, stated that the gem could not be returned to India as the move would set an unworkable precedent: "*If you say yes to one you suddenly find the British Museum would be empty.*" Therefore, for the present moment, the United Kingdom has unilaterally decided to keep the diamond in Britain, even though it was procured via illegitimate means. Iran, Afghanistan and Pakistan have also officially claimed it independently and applied pressure to Britain to give it to them.

The gem remains the property of the British Crown and is kept in HM Tower of London. It is a popular attraction. As the Koh-i-Noor attracts tourists in London, Afghanistan has drawn national intrigue and interference for centuries.

* * *

When the Afghans in Nadir Shah's army returned home after his death in 1747; their leader, Ahmad Shah Abdali, entered Kandahar and was elected king by the Loya Jerga (grand tribal assembly). He was given the title of Durr-e-Durran ('pearl of pearls') and from that time on the name of his tribe was changed to Durrani. For the next twenty five years during his reign the Afghan empire extended from the Amu Darya (Oxus River) in the north to the Arabian Sea and from Herat (a city in western Afghanistan) to Punjab (a province in Pakistan). Ahmad Shah wins from his people the title of Baba (father of the nation). The throne remained in Afghanistan with Ahmad Shah's tribe, though much disputed among his descendants until it ended in 1818.

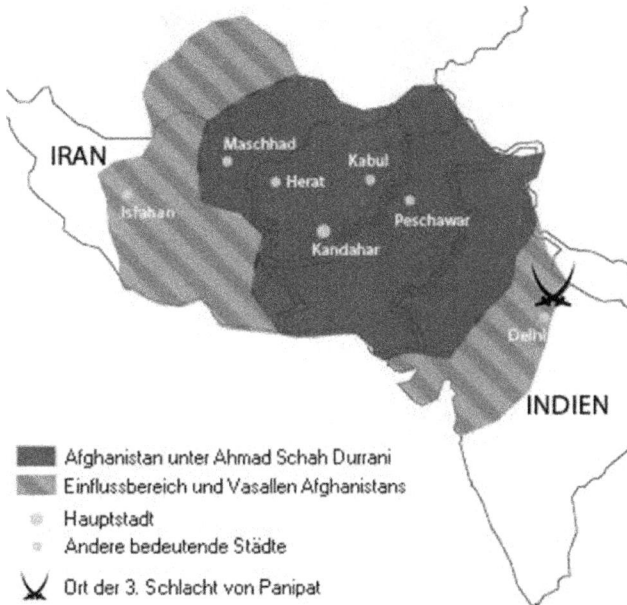

Afghanistan unter Ahmad Schah Durrani
Einflussbereich und Vasallen Afghanistans
Hauptstadt
Andere bedeutende Städte
Ort der 3. Schlacht von Panipat

The Barakzai dynasty was the line of rulers in Afghanistan in the 19th and 20th centuries. Following the fall of the Durrani Empire in 1826, chaos reigned in the domains of Ahmed Shah Durrani's Afghan Empire as various sons of Timur Shah struggled for supremacy. The Afghan Empire ceased to exist as a single nation state, disintegrating for a brief time into a fragmented collection of small units. Dost Mohammad Khan gained preeminence in 1826 and founded the Barakzai dynasty in about 1837, but the struggle for the throne of the country among brothers and cousins of the Barakzai family remained for a few decades, although in time of war against the Great Britain, the unity of the Afghans remained intact.

Amir Dost Mohammad Khan

The in-house fighting continued until Amir Abdul Rahman Khan seized power and became the King of Afghanistan. Abdur Rahman lived in exile in Tashkent, then part of Russian Turkestan, for eleven years.

On July 22, 1880, Abdur Rahman was officially recognized as Amir, granted assistance in arms and money, and promised, in case of unprovoked foreign aggression, such further aid as might be necessary to repel it, provided that he aligned his foreign policy with the British. The British evacuation of Afghanistan was settled on the terms proposed, and in 1881 British troops also handed over Kandahar to the new Amir.

Amir Abdul Rahman Khan

From the end of 1888, the Amir spent eighteen months in his northern provinces bordering upon the Oxus, where he was engaged in pacifying the country that had been disturbed by revolts and in punishing with a heavy hand all who were known or suspected to have taken any part in rebellion.

Shortly afterwards (in 1892) he succeeded in finally beating down the resistance of the Hazara people, who vainly attempted to defend their independence, within their highlands, of the central authority at Kabul. In the late 1880s many of the Hazara tribes revolted against Abdur Rahman, the first ruler to bring the country of Afghanistan under a centralized Afghan government. Consequent on this unsuccessful revolt, numbers of Hazaras fled to Quetta in Balochistan, to the area around Mashhed in northeastern Iran, Russia, Iraq, Tajikistan, Uzbekistan, Azerbaijan, China and India. Most active in the revolt were the Uruzgani, the southernmost of the Hazara tribes. Following their defeat, a considerable number of Uruzgani left the country, as did many Jaghori, their nearest neighbors to the northeast.

In the Shikhali district an estimated 7,000 head of cattle were taken away from Hazaras and 350 men and women of the Jaghori district had been sold at Kabul markets each at the price of 20–21 Afg. Abdur Rahman Khan's brutal suppression compelled a large number of Hazaras to seek refuge in Iran, India, and Russia. Abdur Rahman Khan could only succeed in subjugating Hazaras and conquering their land when he effectively utilized internal differences within the Hazara community, co-opting sold-out Hazara chiefs into his bureaucratic sales of the enslaved Hazara men, women and children in 1897, the Hazaras remained de facto slaves until King Amanulla Khan declared Afghanistan's independence in 1919.

Abdur Rahman died on October 1, 1901, being succeeded by his son Habibulla Khan. He had defeated all enterprises by rivals against his throne; he had broken down the power of local chiefs, and tamed the refractory tribes; so that his orders were irresistible throughout the whole dominion. His government was a military despotism resting upon a well-appointed army; it was administered through officials absolutely subservient to an inflexible will and controlled by a widespread system of espionage; while the exercise of his personal authority was too often stained by acts of unnecessary cruelty.

He held open courts for the receipt of petitioners and the dispensation of justice; and in the disposal of business he was indefatigable. He succeeded in imposing an organized government upon the fiercest and most unruly population in Asia; he availed himself of European inventions for strengthening his armament, while he sternly set his face against all innovations, like railways and telegraph, which might give Europeans a foothold within his country.

His adventurous life, his forcible character, the position of his state as a barrier between the Indian and the Russian empires, and the skill with which he held the balance in dealing with them, combined to make him a prominent figure in contemporary Asian politics and would mark his reign as an epoch in the history of Afghanistan. The Amir received an annual subsidy from the British government of 1,850,000 rupees and was allowed to import munitions of war.

Amir Habibulla Khan and his son, Prince Amanulla Khan

In 1893 Mortimer Durand negotiated with Abdur Rahman Khan, the Durand Line Treaty for the demarcation of the frontier between Afghanistan, the FATA, North-West Frontier Province (NWFP), now named Khybar Pakhtunkhaw, and Baluchistan Provinces of Pakistan the successor state of British India. This line, the Durand Line, is named after him and still remains as an unrecognized boundary by the Government of Afghanistan.

In 1893, Durand was deputed to Kabul by the government of British India for the purpose of settling an exchange of territory required by the demarcation of the boundary between northeastern Afghanistan and the Russian possessions, and in order to discuss with Amir Abdur Rahman Khan other pending questions. Abdur Rahman Khan showed his usual ability in diplomatic argument, his tenacity where his own views or claims were in debate, with a sure underlying insight into the real situation.

In the agreement, the relations between the British Indian and Afghan governments, as previously arranged, were confirmed; and an understanding was reached upon the important and difficult subject of the border line of Afghanistan on the east, towards India.

The area in which the Durand Line lays has been inhabited by the indigenous Pashtuns since ancient time, at least since 500 B.C. The Greek historian Herodotus mentioned a people called Pactyans living in and around Arachosia as early as the 1st millennium B.C. The Baloch tribes inhabit the southern end of the line, which runs in the Balochistan region that separates the ethnic Baloch people.

In 1839, during the First Anglo-Afghan War, British-Indian forces ventured deep into the Pashtun area and began war with the Afghan rulers. Two years later, in 1842, the British were totally defeated and the war ended. The British again invaded Afghanistan in 1878, during the Second Anglo-Afghan War, but withdrew a couple of years later. Mortimer Durand was deputed to Kabul in 1893 by the government of British India for the purpose of obtaining an agreement from Amir Abdur Rahman Khan to mark a line between Afghanistan and British India.

There was no national consensus made in Afghanistan, and a majority of the population was unaware that their native land was planned to be split in half permanently. The resulting Durand Line Agreement or Durand Line Treaty would ensure the carving out of a new province called North-West Frontier Province (NWFP) out of annexed areas from Afghanistan, which are currently part of Pakistan and includes the Federally Administered Tribal Area (FATA) and Frontier Regions. It also included the areas of Multan, Mianwali, the Bahawalpur, and Dera Ghazi Khan. These areas were part of the Afghan Empire from 1747 until around the 1820s when the Sikh, followed by the British, invaded and took possession. They were annexed with the Punjab

Province of Pakistan as late as 1970, after one of the units was dissolved by President Yahya Khan, resulting in a shrunken NWFP.

The British and Russian governments established the boundaries of Afghanistan in such a manner where Afghanistan became a buffer zone between the two empires. This had long-term repercussions that are still being manifested today.

CHAPTER ONE
My Grandfather

General Abdul Ghafar (my grandfather)

The Afghan population was made up of several ethnic groups; the south of the country was predominantly Pashtuns; the central part of the country mostly Hazara, The north was occupied by Uzbeks, Turkmens and Tajeks.

In order to separate the Uzbek, Turkmen and Tajek Afghan citizens from the same ethnic groups who lived on the other side of the border, which was under the control of the Russians, the king wanted to create his own buffer zone by relocating Pashtuns from the south of the country alongside of the northern border. He relocated several tribes from the Pashtun areas of the south by giving them government land.

The king had a royal guard made up of Afghans who were loyal to the King. He also recruited young men from his own Mohammadzai clan to become guards and later officers of the royal court. There were many conditions a young man had to meet to be accepted for the royal guard. Two of the conditions were very important. First, both parents of the young man should be from the Mohammadzai clan, and second he should be introduced by his father to the king.

The king was renovating the Kabul palace and decided to fill the moat, so he brought in the army to do the job. One day the king arrived at the site to inspect the progress of the work and a boy, about 5 ft. 4 inches tall, caught his eye. The boy looked about 13 years old and was carrying a rock almost as big as he was. Impressed by the young man's hard work, the king wanted to reward him with some money. He ordered one of the officers to bring the boy to him. The king asked the young boy, "What's your name boy? Where are you from; who are your family?" The boy answered, "I'm the son of Sardar Shah Mohammad Khan, who is a cousin of the king."

According to the rules at that time, Mohammadzai's should marry only Mohammadzai's. If they wanted to marry from another tribe, it should be by the permission of the king. Shad Mohammad had two wives, one Mohammadzai and the other was from a tribal area. When the king asked for Sardar Shad Mohammad's son to be a guard in the palace, he introduced the son (Amir Mohammad) from his Mohammadzai wife. Abdul Ghafar, who stood before him, who was from Sardar's tribal wife wasn't introduced. The king became upset and asked, "Why did your father not introduce you to me so you can become a royal guard?" The boy didn't answer and later the king finds out his mother wasn't Mohammadzai, but a Pashtun from the Ghelzai tribe.

But the king likes the boy so much he makes him the captain of the young guards in the palace. Later the young man becomes General Abdul Ghafar and the king had so much trust in him he was appointed as the commanding general of the king's army in the northern part of the country. The young general is put in charge of relocating the Pashtuns in the north and allocates federal land to the tribes. He remains in the north under King Habibulla for almost 20 years until Habibulla's son, Amanulla becomes King of Afghanistan.

When Amanulla becomes King after his father's assassination, the young ruler promotes General Ghafar to a higher rank and invites him to Kabul. The general refuses the promotion and does not accept the new king. He sends the king a message; the throne belongs to the king's older brother who is the heir, and he humbly states in his message that out of loyalty and dedication to the royal family it is his duty to warn the young prince not to become king without the consent of the royal family. If he becomes the king without their approval, the kingdom would be finished.

King Amanulla was very upset with the general over this and summons him to his court in Kabul. There he asks the general, with all the good intentions he'd shown, why the general had not accepted him as the king. The general repeats he's been the servant of the previous king and still believes the kingdom should go to the king's older brother, who is heir. If Amanulla does not follow tradition, there would be a split in the family and their rule of the kingdom would be over.

The king got very mad and told him to take his sword out and break it (signifying a dishonorable discharge). The general disobeys by saying that he's earned the sword with honor and service to the king's father and grandfather and he won't do that. That makes the king even angrier and he orders the soldiers to forcefully take Ghafar's sword and put him in the palace jail.

Ghafar was released from jail after a month. The king himself goes to the entrance of the jail, hoping the general would come to him and apologize to get his position back. But that does not happen. The general leaves the palace never to return again. After this incident he changed his lifestyle completely. He bought a humble house in one of the villages near Kabul, called Deh Mazang, away from the residential areas where the Mohammadzai's lived and starts a modest life amongst the farmers and ordinary folks.

One day there was a funeral for a farmer in the village and Ghafar attends. The Afghan custom was to carry the coffin to the grave in turns. At this time the new King of Afghanistan, Nadir Shah, was passing through Deh Mazang on his way to Paghman and Ghafar caught the king's eye. He orders his driver to stop. The king leaves the car and approaches Ghafar and gives his condolences, apologizing for not knowing a family member of his had passed away. Ghafar responds that he appreciates the kings concern, but the funeral is of a neighbor and not a family member. The king asks the general why he does not visit the palace; the kingdom needs distinguished people like him. Promising that Ghafar would have his old rank and position any time he comes. The general tells the king he is still loyal to the family of the late King Amir Abdul Rahman and it would be hypocritical of him to come to the palace and see it occupied otherwise. The king knew Ghafar and respected his loyalty and understood that he wasn't a threat to him, After paying his respects to Ghafar the King leaves to continue his trip to Paghman.

When King Amanulla was ousted and Habibula, the son of a waterman (bache saqa), became king, General Mohammad Nader attacked Kabul from the south with the help of Pashtuns to liberate the country from the rule of bandits. Habibula sends his envoy to persuade General Ghafar to serve and lead the fight against the forces of General Nader. But Ghafar refused; staying true to his allegiance to the family of the king he served

* * *

Ghafar had four children, Abdullah; (my father) was the oldest. When Abdullah was ten years old, his father married him to a nine year old girl, Gouhar Taj (my mother) from another clan of Mohammadzai; she was brought on a chariot (dooli) from another city to Maimana. My mother's lineage traces back to the four Kandahari brothers who were the rulers of Kandahar. My mother's great-grandfather was the oldest, Sardar Kohandell Khan.

My father's lineage traces back to the Pashawari Sardars who ruled the Provinces of Punjab; my father's great grandfather was Sardar peer Mohammad Khan, the youngest brother of Sardar Sultan Mohammad Khan who was the great grandfather of the Late King Mohammad Zahir Shaw. My grandfather married my father to another girl, a Mohammadzai, when he was only fourteen, without his consent or presence, and he divorced her, without Abdullah's presence or consent after nine months.

My father told me my grandfather was a disciplined man in home as well as in his work. Once when still a general he commanded a small army (compared to those of the neighboring countries in the north). When the Khan of Turkmenistan visited Maimana, according to my father, in order to show the Khan his army was a large one, my grandfather prepared different uniforms for his soldiers and in a parade for the Khan he passed the same soldiers twice.

Another story my father told me about him was at dinner he always had many people from all walks of life eat with him (there were no tables; they put a long large cloth on the floor, called *destsrkhan* and people sat around it and ate with their hands.) The dinner consisted of a variety of delicacies and rice dishes. He would start by taking three large handful of rice and a piece of bread and when he finished it, he signaled the servers to take everything away. He'd announce to his dinner guest that over-eating makes a man sick and lazy. The guests and everyone at the dinner would then go hungry.

Grandfather was a small man but in very good shape. His desire to keep not only himself disciplined but his surroundings as well spilled over to government. Maimana had a governor, who was appointed by the king to do all the civilian duties for the kingdom, but Ghafar was an active military officer that did not recognize the authority of the governor; he actually took control of civil duties of the government as well as military.

In Deh Mazang, Ghafar and four of his children, his only wife, his son's wife (my mother), and eight slaves lived until he passed away at age 70.

CHAPTER TWO
My Father

Abdullah Ghafar (my father)

There is a candle in your heart... (by Rumi)
Translated by Sharam Shiva

There is a candle in your heart,
  ready to be kindled.
There is a void in your soul,
  ready to be filled.
You feel it, don't you?
You feel the separation

from the Beloved.
Invite Him to fill you up,
   embrace the fire.
Remind those who tell you otherwise that
   Love comes to you of its own accord,
   and the yearning for it
   cannot be learned in any school.

My father Abdullah, unlike his father, was not a military man. He committed all of his life to learning and became the head of the family after his father's death. Abdullah's younger brother Sharif was sent to military school at the age of nine, and died after a short illness. He had two sisters; one was married to her cousin, Hider Naysan who became a famous poet. The other sister married a man who was the grandson of Prince Kamran from the Durrani dynasty.

Abdullah was a top student in his class and graduated from Habibia High School (at that time the highest level of education). People were encouraged to go to school. King Amanulla himself believed in education and was personally teaching a class at the high school.

My father was appointed district governor of Hazarajat at age 18 and later graduated from the first college in Kabul while working in the ministry of public works. After he got his degree in law school, he was appointed to the court system and was a part of the office of the prime minister. When Mohammad Dawoud became prime minister, he promoted him to become the deputy auditor (comptroller), and later became a judge in the appeals court. Later on in his life, he became a member of the supreme court of Afghanistan when the judicial system was modeled after the US

Unlike his father, he left all the domestic affairs of the family in my mother's care, and put all of his efforts in his work. As much as he was a very capable judge and administrator, he was not as skilled in his personal financial affairs. If it were not for the inheritance left from his father, he would have been broke. Anytime he ran out of money, he would sell a piece of the land. My mother was the one who took charge of everything and, being illiterate, she would do things in a traditional way; no investing or saving.

Unlike the traditional Afghans who punished their children by beating, my father never beat me, except one time. I cut a small beautiful tree in the yard to make a pretend sword out of it and play movies with my friends. At that time Indian movies were very popular in Kabul and we liked to play movie heroes with our swords. Mahipal was a very famous Indian movie hero, and I was playing the role of Mahipal fighting four other kids who were about three years younger than me. I was 11 years old and chasing the others around the yard. When they chased me I climbed on the roof, through a window which was in the outhouse. When I decided to come down, I used the same window in the outhouse to come down, but not being able to see where I was landing, I ended up inside the hole, totally drenched in human waste. I came out of the hole with a lot difficulty and all the kids laughing at me. My mother came and she could not stop laughing either. After cleaning up, my father came home from work and found out that I cut the tree. On top of humiliation and embarrassment of falling in the outhouse hole, I got a few slaps in my face from him for damaging the tree. My younger brother, who lives in the United States now too, told the story to my kids and they still laugh about it.

I was my father's favorite son, and since education was very important to him I never failed and got good grades. Although at times I just did enough to pass and make it to next year's class. But I still showed interest in learning and would stay up with him till late at night, because he did not want to eat till 10:00PM. Other kids were fed earlier and went to bed, but I stayed with my dad. He was amazingly talented at teaching me about family history, world history, classical traditional music and different kinds of ragas (music from India, which I hated at that time). Although he was not a religious man, he had memorized the whole Koran when he was young and would discuss the different parts and compare its applicability with the modern world. That is one of the reasons I know my family history and the untold history of the country better than all of my family members.

He was a true patriot and very much a man who believed in monarchy and aristocracy. Later on when I was in higher grades, much influenced by my street friends and not fond of the system of monarchy, I would argue with him, but he never got mad or stated that my opinions were wrong. He would add that for a country like Afghanistan, in his opinion monarchy was the best, and above all he said that the then current rulers were very smart to keep the foreigners out of the country by being neutral. He admitted that the education system and economy could have been much better if the government paid more attention, but he said that he preferred peace and security and keeping the foreign powers out of the country more than economic progress. He said if the government allows one foreign power in the country it makes the other foreign powers alarmed and envious and that would divide the country and start a civil war. Of course I disagreed with him at all times.

One of the things that I regret for the rest of my life is that I was not able to see him again after I left the country. He was disappointed in me at the beginning, but later he understood. I really wanted to see him, and for him to see my children. But I could not go for fear of my life and he did not want to come and live outside of his beloved country, and be dependent on me or anybody else. He was too proud to have someone have to care for him.

My father's influence: his honesty, humbleness, the importance he placed on education and his teaching of history to me were monumental in my life.

CHAPTER THREE
My Early Years

I was born in Deh Mazang, (a village near Kabul) the fifth son of my father Abdullah. My parents had ten children. Nine sons; one died at the age of nine and another at two years old, and two adopted sisters. My oldest brother was 23 years older than me. If he were alive today he would be 92 years old; he was only 14 years younger than my father.

There were four high schools in the whole capital. Habibia High School was the oldest and first opened during the time of King Habibulla, and it is named after him. The Americans took control of the school and provided assistance in terms of teachers and financial support. The principal of the school was an American, and there were other American teachers; for English, Physics, Chemistry, and Math. Nejat High School, was run by Germans, Isteqlal High School was run by French, and Ghazi High School by the English. At age six I was a student at Habibia High School, which was a combined school that included elementary, intermediate and high school.

After a year my father moved us to a new and more prestigious residential section of Kabul called Shar-e-Naw. My school was not changed and I finished all 12 years of school at Habibia.

For the first grade my mother would send one of the servants with me to sit outside of the classroom until school was finished. At the end of the school day I either walked home with him or another servant would come with a horse-drawn carriage to pick us both up. The first bus service started later, when I was in fourth grade. The Afghan school system was totally different from that in United States. Besides learning how to read and write we had to learn about religion by memorizing chapters from the Koran and about prayers and the five pillars of Islam. The teachers from that early age would discipline us. I was always worried about my homework, and was scared that I would be punished if I did not memorize all the chapters of Koran. My adopted sister was a very bright girl and loved me. She was also my roommate, and stayed till late at night to help me do my homework. My parents were very proud of me, even at that early age, because my brothers, who were older than me, did not show much interest in school. My parents were always on them to take more interest. But I liked school and was always encouraged in a positive way to continue my education.

When my grandfather died he left my father (in addition to thousand acres of land in Maimana and on the outskirts of Kabul), about a 1,000 gold coins buried under his bed. My father invested the majority of it in First Afghan Bank (the only bank available, which at that time had just been started) and bought stocks as well. He used some of the money to buy three parcels of land in Shar-e-Naw to build three houses, one for each of my older brothers who were already married and one big one for the rest of us.

My oldest brother was married when he was in 8th grade. He absolutely hated school. No matter what my father did, he would not try to do better in school. So he failed every year, until they kicked him out. A friend of my father knew that he (my father) had many properties and was considered wealthy. He proposed that if my father allowed my brother to marry his daughter, he would persuade my brother to finish school. Out of desperation my father agreed, because he wanted his first son to follow him and become educated. But he failed.

The second oldest brother did finish all 12 years of school, but it took 17 years. He ran away with one of my cousins, got married without the consent of my father, then came back and lived with us and continued going to school.

The third oldest brother did not like school either. He was very intelligent but got involved with gangs to the embarrassment of my father. Despite that my father sent him to Maimana to take charge of the land we had there. He was married to a girl, from the Mohammadzai family, when he was only sixteen and had 10 children.

He finished high school and went on to the college of engineering and became an engineer, and later mayor of Maimana. When the communists took over they searched for and tried to kill him, but he escaped with all of his children to Germany. I sponsored him to become an American citizen; he now commutes between his home in Maimana and Las Vegas, where he settled with his family.

After we moved to Shar-e-Naw, we lived in a large, modern home with a very big yard full of flowers, fruit trees and vines and plenty of space to play sports. Unlike most of the other Mohammadzai's kids who played and hung around their own family clans, I had friends from the street from different ethnic and religious groups. I felt uncomfortable around my own cousins and relatives. As much as my father was an aristocrat, I was not. I did not go to my aunts or any other relative's house and spent most of my time with my street friends who were very hard working and smart students. Their fathers were not as influential or rich like mine. My parents however never told me not to hang out with my friends and actually liked them. My friends were polite and spent a lot of time with me. We studied, played cards and soccer. My parents never told me to do homework or study or to come home at a specific time. I stayed out till relatively late and did what I wanted to do with my friends. The bad experience my parents had with my brothers, being strict with them and pushing them to study only to fail was not something they wanted to repeat with me. They chose another method: they did not stop me from what I was doing and allowed me quite a bit of freedom for a young boy—as long as I did well in school.

I was a top student from 1st grade till 6th grade. In 7th grade I started to not pay much attention to school. It was not girls or drugs or any of the things that gets some young kid's attention here in United States; for me it was sports and movies.

Going to the movies was one of the luxuries of my teenage years. There were five or six movie theaters in Kabul. Four of them showed Indian movies all the time and the majority of people identified with them. Two cinemas showed American movies and these theaters were very popular among young educated people. My friends and I always went to the Park Theater. It was close to our house and we occasionally ventured to the Ariana, which was farther (many kilometers walked to get there) and was next to a western style restaurant called Khyber. But every Thursday night we went to the Park. Since we knew the person in the ticket office, he would keep the same seats for us that night. If we did not go we would let him know ahead of time, which did not happen very often.

My most beautiful memories of going to the cinema were during winter. When we came out of the movie to snow covered roads and only a few cars around the theater to disturb it—it was like a new world. We'd go to a kabob house and then walk home on dark streets with snow coming in flakes larger than I have seen anywhere in the world. Except once when I went skiing in Davos, Switzerland, there I saw the same kind of snowflakes. It made me nostalgic for my teenage years in Kabul.

During summer we biked to Shamali, where the king had a swimming pool in Kariz-e-Meer for the public. Sometimes, even during school days, a bunch of us would skip school and ride our bikes through the mountain pass at Kotal-e-Khyr Khana (which was about 8,000 feet high) to the Shamali plains, about 30 kilometers from home. We biked just to spend the day swimming. Climbing through the pass was hard, but we found a way to make it easier. We brought ropes with us from home and when a very slow moving truck was in front of us (and most were slow for two reasons: they were overloaded and the pass was very steep), we'd throw a rope and catch a truck latch and let the truck pull us to the top. If the truck stopped, then we released the rope and started peddling.

After 9th grade, at times I would get sick of school. I'd take a little "vacation" and give my notebooks to my friend and tell him to take notes for me as well as himself, and make sure I was not marked absent. The teachers did not have a roll call. When we first came to school we all had a formation, and the captain of the class would call roll, and if you knew the captain, you would never be marked absent. There was not a tradition where the teachers would call your parents, for a teacher, parent, or student conference. My father had never met any of my teachers.

The teachers and principal would always have a stick in their hands as a deterrence or if need be, to punish the students. That was the rule and everybody accepted it. Teachers were respected by parents as well as students. Sometimes if students went home with a swollen face or swollen hands because the teacher beat him; the parents instead of getting mad at the teacher would get mad at their kid, saying the teacher must have had a good reason to beat them.

There were two other swimming pools in Kabul; one in Bagh-e-Babur and one in Breshnakot. The Breshnakot swimming pool was made by the Germans, who were working on power generation around Kabul. One of my friends father worked for the ministry of mining and got us written permission from the Germans to swim there. His father studied in Germany, and knew many Germans in Kabul.

The other swimming pool was in Babur gardens, which were made for King Babur the Mongol Dynasty's king who ruled India, and Afghanistan. In 1525 Babur, a descendant of Timur, rose to power and made Kabul the capital of his Moghul Empire. From the 16th century to the early 18th century Afghanistan was divided into three major parts. The north was recognized as the Kingdom of Balk, which was ruled by Uzbeks Khans, the west was under Persian Safavid rule and the east belonged to the Moghuls. There was constant war fought over the region of Kandahar, at times it was taken over by the Mughals but most of the time was ruled by the Persians. Babur conquered most cities of Afghanistan before his campaign in India. In the city of Kandahar his personal inscriptions can be found in the Chilzina rock mountain. It is said that he didn't have enough time to finish before news came about a Persian advance from the west. In hearing this he and his army quickly left the area. Instead of looking towards Persia, the Moghul Empire was more focused on the Indian subcontinent, which included the region known as Kabulistan. Babur Shah loved Kabul and made it his summer capital. The poet explains Kabul to actually be named "Gabul," in Persian (because it was so beautiful) the name came from combining two words, after a drop of dew or water on a flower: Ab for *aab* – water, inside a *Gul* – flower.

We would also go to Qargha, a beautiful lake about 2 kilometers in length, about 20 kilometers from Kabul and to Paghman, a mountainside resort, about 30 kilometers from Kabul. Paghman was uphill all the way. The temperature difference was about 15 degrees centigrade, and the altitude was probably 9,000 to 10,000 ft. above sea level. We rented a room for 10 to 15 of us. We'd cook for ourselves and one of my friends would play the accordion—we'd eat and sit listening to music, playing cards and telling jokes.

I still remember those wonderful days and nights. On weekends we went to a hill top, owned by the king, but open to public. It had a swimming pool as well with a civilian gardener as a guard. We paid him a few Afghanis and he would let us swim until midnight. Of course the king would never come there when the public was around.

On Thursday's and Friday's (and other holidays) many Afghan families come to Paghman to picnic. We would find a place next to a family with pretty daughters and start our music hoping to get the girls attention. And if we made an eye contact then we fell in 'love' with that girl. Openly dating was out of question, although it was done quietly.

During winter, when school was closed, I would also go with my friends to Jalalabad, close to the Pakistan border. Jalalabad, located at sea level unlike Kabul, was warm during winters, no snow at all and temperatures way above freezing. We would always rent only one room for all of us, and do the same things as at Paghman. During the day we'd hike to different villages and one day we came to a river. My friends wanted to turn back but I insisted that we cross this river. It wasn't deep or fast, so I thought it no problem but nobody agreed with me. I said, "I will go first." If I can't make it I'll turn back, if I make it then you can follow me." They all agreed to that. One of my friends, my classmate who I had shared a bench for years in school, also the shortest boy in our bunch, said that he couldn't let me go alone. We both started to cross, and the water quickly came almost to our shoulders. We made it without drowning or being washed off of our feet but the rest did not follow us.

Amir still remains my best friend. He comes from a family who was the spiritual leaders of Shiia Afghans and lived in the Chendawol section of Kabul. This was a historical section of Kabul where mostly the Shia Afghans lived and some of the most brilliant Afghans come from that neighborhood. Amir and I became friends after fighting over a bench in fifth grade. We both wanted to reserve that bench and then invite someone we knew to share it with us. Neither one of us wanted to give up, so decided to share it. We got along so well that we sat together for another eight years. The schools in Afghanistan are very different from the United States. We didn't change rooms for different subjects. We stayed in the same room and different teachers came to the classroom. This was also true for students, if you did not fail a year, almost all students would stay together in same class, until they graduated. After high school, Amir went to medical school and I went to the military academy, but we never lost touch. He would come to see me on Thursdays in the academy, and on Fridays, Amir, I and all of our other friends would spend the day together.

***

After I left Afghanistan for the United States, he got involved with the communists and became very active. The group he belonged to, mostly intellectuals was trying to bring equality and justice to the country. He became a very important person in their inner circle, and later, when communists took over the country, he became the Minister of Public Health. He is the only communist I know who was not an opportunist.

When he was appointed as the chief of Wazeer Akbar Khan hospital in the time of President Dawoud, I sent him a letter to congratulate him on his new position. He replied questioning my patriotism for not returning home. I did not like the way the letter sounded, I thought he had become like the other communists; forgetting what they were fighting for, and discriminating against people who did not join their way of thinking. I wrote him back and stated that since I was a

Mohammadzai, and not a communist, he should stop going to my parent's house and to cut all ties with me. And that if he didn't do that, it might hurt his career with his party. But he never stopped paying his respects to my father and mother. He visited them every Friday and made sure nobody bothered them, and he helped my two younger brothers with their visas and departure from Afghanistan.

Years went by and I had no contact with him. Until a friend of mine flying for a Middle Eastern airline, told me that he saw my friend in Yemen and that he was the Afghanistan ambassador to Yemen. This was around the time that Dr. Najeeb was falling and the Mujahidin were taking control of Afghanistan. I found Amir's telephone number and called him. I talked to him for a long time. He had orders from Kabul to sell the embassy, close it and return to Afghanistan. He wanted to do that and return home but I advised him to go to the American embassy and apply for political asylum. I offered to help by sponsoring him or whatever he needed. He laughed and told me that after many years of friendship, I still did not know him very well. He said a few days before my call he had challenged the American ambassador on some international issues. How could I allow myself to even think that just to save himself he would abandon his beliefs and ideals and go to the American embassy and act like a traitor by asking for asylum? Amir remained in Yemen for a while and did not return to Afghanistan. The Norwegian government gave him refuge and that is where he lives. I visited him there and from what others told me, in Yemen and Afghanistan, he never hurt anyone and rejected any position which would require him to directly or indirectly hurt or interrogate people. He has not changed his beliefs and is still my best childhood friend.

My trip to Bamyan

One summer the temperature got to around 40 degrees Celsius (104 Fahrenheit) the schools closed because we had no air conditioning and students were fainting right and left. My three friends and I decided to go to Bamyan by bicycle. I did not have a bicycle and borrowed a bike from another friend.

All of us were around 16 years old, had never travelled that far by ourselves, did not have any experience and wanted to travel almost 150 kilometers on a dirt road through mountain passes around 9,000 ft. high. We started at 9.00PM got to Charekar and slept in a tea house. We covered the only paved road toward Bamyan and my friend Hedayat (who is a senior minister in Karzai's cabinet now), had his father's pistol in his pocket, just in case anyone bothered us. We got up the next morning for the rest of the treacherous journey toward Bamyan which took us several days. When we were walking our bikes on Shebar Pass, in the Hindukosh Mountains, my friends cursed me, because the trip was my idea. We all cried out of exhaustion but finally climbed the pass, and on the other side saw the beautiful mountains and river flowing between them. This eased the pain a little.

We reached the road where a bridge led toward Bamyan valley and another toward Duaab (two waters). The ride to Bayman from this point was not that long as I remember it. We reached the town after a few hours and went to the only hotel and stayed there at night. In the morning we started our tour at Shahr-e-Ghoghola (the city of noise). They told us it was destroyed by Genghis Khan. The city had a canal system for water from some underground source, and was well-established. The legend says it was under siege for many months until the princess of the city, who was in love with the prince of the invaders, gave him the secret of the underground water system and thus the city fell.

The valley also contained the world's largest statues of Buddha. They are located on what is described as the roof of the world at 9,200 feet; it is the geographical heart of Asia and crossroad of the Western and Eastern ancient civilizations. It was the cultural capital of ancient civilizations and trade; the axis of the Silk Road trade. The beautiful valley lies amidst the mountainous highlands of Hindu Kush and Pamir. Center of the ancient Kushan Empire, Bamyan centuries ago used to be an intersection where Eastern and Western civilizations met and co-existed as a center of trade between East and West. Bamyan has a rich history of civilization, but also tragic memories of brutality.

Travelers and conquerors have appreciated the beauty of this valley, which not only impressed Marco Polo, but also Alexander the Great.

Next day we climbed the head of both majestic Buddha's. The view of the valley from the head was breath taking and the frescos around it were magnificent. We spent the whole day in the ruins and climbing through the different caves that were originally built for monks for meditation. Now several of them were used by local Hazara's as dwellings and sadly, the Buddha's were destroyed by the Taliban on March 11, 2001. The local people are ancestors of the builders of the Buddhas (who once followed Buddhism before the rise of Islam in this region) and they remember that as a black day.

The next day, I came up with another idea, to go to Band-e-Amir. It's claimed that this lake is one of the natural wonders of the world. Recently the Afghan government declared Band-e-Amir as the first national park in Afghanistan. The distance from Bamyan and Bad-e-Amir was only about 75 kilometers, but the road is very primitive and dangerous with high passes.

We started early in the morning, all four of us. We were about 10 kilometers away from Bamyan when Sami's bike (Sami is a medical doctor who lives in Oklahoma now) got a flat. We fixed the flat but he refused to put another foot toward Band-e-Amir. Hedayat, Yaseen and I did not agree with him, we were going to finish what we started and kept on riding. The temperature was unbearable. We did not have food or water, but we kept going. We reached a point where we could not go any further because of thirst. We searched to find a village to ask for water and food, without success. We climbed another relatively shallow pass and saw a number of nomad tents. Hedayat speaks Pashtu perfectly (it is his mother tongue), so he took the lead and headed towards the tents. The Kochi dogs barked at us and a few nomads showed up. Hedayat started talking to them and we were invited inside. Water, buttermilk and rice were brought for us and we were treated like kings in the tradition of real Pashtun hospitality. We rested for a while, and despite my friends' suggestion to turn back, I insisted we go forward until we reached Band-e-Amir.

We said good bye to our new nomad friends and again started toward Band-e-Amir. Hours passed and we could not see the lakes. Around sunset, suddenly we saw a breathtaking series of lakes to our right. We were very excited at that but there was nothing around the lake, except a mosque on the other side of the main lake. By looking around we found out that we had to pass under one dam, which is called Band-e-Haybat, and that would put us on the side of the dam by the Mosque.

Band-e Amir is a series of six deep blue lakes separated by natural dams made of travertine, a mineral deposit. The lakes are situated in the Hindu Kush Mountains of Central Afghanistan at approximately 3000 meters (9000 ft.) of elevation, west of the famous Buddha's of Bamiyan.

They were created by the carbon dioxide rich water oozing out of the faults and fractures to deposit calcium carbonate precipitate in the form of travertine walls that today store the water of these lakes. Band-e Amir is one of the few rare natural lakes in the world which are created by travertine systems, all of which are on UNESCO World heritage list. In 2009, Band-e Amir became Afghanistan's first national park.

To Lift a Mirror, for What You've Lost

Band-e-Amir

We got to the other side as night was falling and the weather getting cold. All we had were our bikes and nothing else. The mosque did not have any doors and not even a roof. I remember sitting there and being blamed by my friends for their discomfort. All of a sudden we saw, as if God sent, a caravan of jeeps; four of them coming our way.

"Oh MY God, is that you Nangy, Hedayat, and Yaseen. What on earth are you kids doing and how did you get here?"

They were Mr. Canfield, our English teacher, Mr. Gets, Math teacher, Mr. Gringo, another English teacher and their wives. They came here to camp because of the heat in Kabul. They fed us, housed us gave us blankets and we sat around the camp fire with them for a good portion of the night. Morning came and we waited until the water was a little warmer to take a swim in the lake before we returned to Bamyan and joined our friend, who we had left behind, for our return trip to Kabul.

The legend says that Band-e-Amir ('Band' means 'Dam' and 'Amir' means 'king' in Dari) was built by Caliph Ali (who is the highest saint of Shia Muslims) in a miracle. The river flooded every year and killed thousands of residents downstream. At this time the legendary Caliph Ali showed up in this part of the world on his horse with his double edged sword. The people of the area recognized him and sent cheese and podeena (a type of herb) to him and asked for his help to calm the wild river. Caliph Ali threw the cheese across the river and a dam was magically built out of the cheese. Then he threw the herb and Band-e-Podeena was built to bring the flood under control. He drew his sword and cut away part of the mountain and placed it in front of the river, from this Band-e-Haybat was formed and the people were saved from flood for eternity.

My trips to Maimana (now called Faryab province)

Schools in Afghanistan have their vacation during winter due to cold weather and lack of facilities. School starts at the beginning of spring and finishes at the end of fall. My father had a lot of land in the north of the country, which he inherited from his father. Married at age nine, my mother was illiterate (unlike my aunts who were schooled, my mother was never allowed by my grandfather to go to school), although she was taught how to run a household and was a great cook. After my grandfather's death, my father was the head of the family. But my mother was the person we all depended on. She managed the family finances and had complete control of all the properties. She took us with her to Maimana during the winter where she would collect the revenues from the harvest and had the servant's dry tomatoes, and eggplants and pickle vegetables all winter to bring back to Kabul.

When we went to Maimana (I started going there when I was eight or nine years old), since there were no buses or airplane, we had to travel in trucks that carried cargo. My mother and young brothers sat in cabin of the truck with the driver, where it was warm, but the other passengers, my Laula (servant who raised me), and I, sat on top of the loads in the back of the trucks exposed to the elements. At times it would snow, or rain and temperatures went below zero. It would take us two days to get to Mazar (now it takes only five hours) and the only road was unpaved road. It went through Shebar Pass and at times, all passengers had to get off the truck, because of the heavy load and steep slope. The poor assistant of the driver (kleenar) who had wooden chocks in his hand would have to quickly place them under the back tires, if the truck started slipping. The passengers who rode on top of the load had no communication with the driver of the truck. If you had to go to the bathroom, you yelled; chances were that the driver did not hear it 95% of the time. Once I had to go to the bathroom very badly. No matter how much I yelled nobody heard, so one of the passengers told me go ahead urinate on the side of a box and hopefully it would not get to the raisins inside.

My brother, Aziz was sent by my Father to Maimana to be in charge of the land and property, because he was not behaving properly in Kabul and failing every grade. I had a soft spot for him and him for me. He gave me one of his horses and every year by the time I got to Maimana that horse was in the best shape. I loved Maimana. Every day I would cross three rivers until I got to town and spent all day either watching Buzkashi (sometimes getting inside the game and running around with the Buzkash's) or riding my horse with other friends toward the hills.

Buzkashi, "bozkashi" is one of the ancient games played in Afghanistan. The name of this game is perhaps derived from hunting mountain goats by ancient champions on horseback. The bozkashi horses possess special qualities. For instance, when the rider falls off the horse, it waits there for the horseman to mount it again. The price of such horses range between Afg. 20,000 and Afg. 100,000 (pre-war prices). Those who train the horses feed them special food at regular intervals. A few days prior to a game, the trainer keeps the horse hungry for part of the day and rides it daily a fairly long distance. This is meant to soften the horse and make it slightly lean to avoid bursting when under excessive strains. The horsemen call their animals after their natural color. For instance, a grey horse is called "taragh", an ash blond horse is referred to as "samand", a red one as "jayran" and a white one as "qezel" or "boze".

The landscape in Maimana is unlike the rest of Afghanistan which is either mountainous or desert; Maimana is a series of hills and fertile soil. During late winter and early spring it is heaven on earth. All of the hills are covered with greenery and wild tulips with different colors.

The village (where my family land is located) is called Kariz Qala, which means (kind of) the 'Spring Castle'. At that time all the houses in the village belonged to us and everyone who lived there were our sharecroppers. When I found out what sharecropper meant (it was explained to me that they cultivate the land with their own seeds, work all year for the harvest, and at the end get 1/5 of the whole harvest) even at that time I thought it was robbery, My father wanted to change it but the other land owners who were mostly local Uzbeks would be very upset to break their tradition.

The house my grandfather built in Kariz Qala was inside high walls with a huge wooden door and rooms with a dome roof made out of dirt (mud). On one side was the residential section; next to it was storage for wheat and other commodities. On the far side were stables for the horses and cows and by the door were the servant quarters. In the morning the servants brought fresh milk, yogurt, eggs and freshly baked bread for us.

My brother converted a huge storage room into a guest room with a dome ceiling and mud walls. During winter a wooden stove was placed in the center of the room for heat and also to cook hashish. I loved this room. A farmer by the name of Khederby would come to this room and play the *Damboora* (a two string musical instrument) for me almost every night and I loved how he played. When he took a break, he would take some kind of a powder out of his pocket and cook it on the fire and mix it in the palm of his hand. Then put it in a water pipe and he would go outside with my brother and smoke it. They would not smoke it inside because of me, but I knew it was hashish. My brother grew it on his land; the farmers extracted the powder from the plant and made hashish out of it and fed the cows the leaves. Now I know why those cows were walking zigzag after they were fed the leaves.

The kids in the village, who were my age, were home during the winter, because they did not have to work in the fields. They were my friends and we would explore and climb the hills inside our property. When we rode farther out from the village I was on my horse and they rode their donkeys. The memories of the beautiful hills of Maimana, where my friends and I rolled from their tops to their bottom, and the wild tulips, are unforgettable. I consider Maimana to be my birth place.

The wild tulips of Maimana

More about school

I was the top student until I got to 7th grade. Then, while school was not a problem as far as learning was concerned, I played more and studied less. I would skip school on warm days and go to the swimming pool in Babur Gardens, or catch a movie at 10.00AM and often would not come back to school for the 5th period.

My street friends were more disciplined than me; they had to go home and do chores. They were worried and did not want me to fail and be separated from them. Every year before the beginning of final exams, they would come to my house and study with me. And that was the only time I would study seriously so that I would pass and we would all graduate at the same year.

My senior year I studied very hard from the beginning and got very good grades. The majority of my friends were Shiite Muslims. They were not allowed to join the military or work in the Ministry of Foreign Affairs, only rich kids or kids with family ties with the ruling family could get scholarships or were allowed to go abroad and study, I thought this unfair. I wanted to go to law school just like my father; become a diplomat, work at the ministry and go abroad. We watched many American movies and I had this dream of travelling outside of Afghanistan to learn new things and coming back to help my poor country. Just like my father (who was the most honest man I know and worked hard all his life), I was going to be the same type of man. My father was a great and honest judge, he never took bribes. If it were not for the wealth my grandfather left him, he would not have survived financially.

CHAPTER FOUR
After High School & Military College

I graduated from high school with my childhood friends and we were very excited to go to Kabul University. Amir, my bench mate who sat next to me from 4th grade to 12th grade went on to medical school, my three other close friends went to engineering school. My name was not on the list of any of the colleges, but soon I heard that the prime minster of the country handpicked me and some other students to go to the military academy to become officers. This was a shock to me, I went to my father who was working directly with the prime minister and asked him to get me out of this mess. But he knew that the prime minister would not make any exception. There were many reasons why this group was chosen; I was chosen because of my grandfather's reputation as a general and my father's honesty and for being a Mohammadzai. I am sure the other students were chosen because of similar reasons.

While I was growing up and throughout school years I dreamed of going abroad, especially to America to study. Those dreams hit a road block when I found out that I was drafted to become an officer in the Afghan Army.

The prime minister wanted to modernize the military forces by bringing the urbanites into the officer corps. Up to that time, most of the officers were from tribal areas of the country. Most of these officers were conservative and loyal to the King. They came to military school when they were seven years old and after finishing military high school they entered the military academy and became officers. Dawoud Khan wanted to bring young urban people into the army not just to modernize it as we were told, but also for his own purposes as I found out later. I had no choice but to report to military academy which was in Bala Hissar palace.

Bala Hissar has a historical significance of its own. It is a beautiful ancient fortress which is nicely located right in the middle of Kabul. The walls of Kabul are about 12 feet thick and about 20 feet high. Constructed during the 5th Century B.C., the Kuh-e-Sherdarwaza Mountain also was close by. This Bala Hissar continues up the mountain ridge to the river. To enter the fortress there are various gates. In the lower part of the fortress there are three royal palaces and barracks as well as the stables. In the upper part of Bala Hissar is the dungeon of Kabul known as Black Pit and the armory. In the 19th Century during the First Anglo-Afghan War during the Second Anglo-Afghan War, the bloodiest fighting was at Bala Hissar, as well. The British from 1839 used it as their barracks. The British Residency during the Second Anglo-Afghan War was burned down here. Later on the Afghan military academy was established at this historical site and new barracks were built for cadets. In 1979, an incident known as the uprising at Bala Hissar by the Afghanistan Liberation Organization was also organized at the site.

I remember the first day I had to report at 5.00AM in the morning and walked from Shar-e-Naw to Bala Hissar that morning. I had on the military uniform I was issued a week previous. When I got to school, the first order was to go to the barbershop and cut our hair.

***

I was envious of my friends and disappointed with where I ended up. I thought my future was ruined and I was going to be the servant of one person (the king). I thought, my only job would be to protect him from his own people, right or wrong, and not be able to serve my people and country. This was the main reason that I did not return home from the United States after my second tour (more on this later in the book).

While I was in the academy my other friends from the civilian high schools were in colleges of their choice. I was demoralized and hated every minute at the academy. At the same time I was joking about it all and was trying to challenge everything. I would do anything to survive mentally, no matter what, and to not let it bother me.

To Lift a Mirror, for What You've Lost

At the academy the city cadets were not liked. Tribal cadets who came from the military high school called us the spoiled kids. They thought we were not tough enough. They wouldn't socialize with us at first and the school had our classes separate from them at the beginning, but later we were mixed.

The senior cadets wanted to make things hard on us intentionally. For example they would assign us watches in the middle of the night to make it hard for us get enough sleep. We were punished for little things (to us, not knowing any better) that we were not familiar with: like not saluting a cadet who was one year ahead of us or if we did not have our head shaved every week. When we were punished there were different types of punishments: spend one night in a cold tent with no bed, or for city kids, no Friday off to go home, or to crawl on your elbows and knees the length of the drill courts (which was about a quarter of a mile). When you were finished your knees and elbows were bloody. But I found a solution to that. I had my Mother sew four cushions (pads) for my knees and elbows and inserted them in my pants and jacket. When I was punished I would finish first and not get bloody. It worked great until I got caught and lost the pads to the sergeant. I took everything as a challenge.

This was the first time in my life that I slept in a barracks with bunk beds, and was not able to leave the premises until Thursday night. We had to wake up at 4.00AM and stand in line to go to the bathrooms. Most students went to the mosque and prayed, and then we assembled. Our breakfast was tea, dark bread and jelly. The bread was made in a bakery that the Russians built for Afghans. The building was the tallest building in Kabul at only five stories tall. But the jelly was contracted by a local man, who brought the jelly early in the morning on his donkey. In the morning when we went to the bathroom, we always saw the donkey, but not the donkey driver, so we all assumed that the guy must have trained his donkey, or the donkey knew the way so well, that every morning, the contractor put the containers of the jelly on the donkey, and directed it toward the academy. That might have been the truth, but it was a laugh for us.

After breakfast, the classes would start. Although the time that I attended the academy was the hardest time of my early adult life and I hated it; the discipline that I learned from the experience stayed with me all my life. I am glad that I went through it.

CHAPTER FIVE
My Transfer to the Afghan Air Force
& First Trip to the United States

There was a rumor that the newly established Royal Afghan Air Force was sending cadets chosen from the academy to the United States for pilot training. The next day we were called to formation in front of the H.Q. to honor the Chief of the Air Force. The chief made a speech and went through the line, choosing cadets just by look and told them that they were going to the United States to become the future fighter pilots for the Afghan Air Force. My friend Jamil and I were looking for a break to get out of the military academy, but were not chosen. We were both disappointed, but it wasn't over yet. Jamil knew a teacher who was related to the chief and begged him to go to the chief and ask him to come back to the academy and choose us. A week later, General Abdul Razaq Khan returned to the Academy and picked both of us. We were transferred from the ground forces of the Afghan Army to the Afghan Air Force.

After a five month wait we were taken to the American Embassy for tests with equipment that the American attaché had brought from the United States to check basic coordination of hands and feet. Then they performed the medical screening. After those tests were finished we received our visas and were fitted for clothes and other necessities. In December of 1960 we flew to Frankfurt Germany where we spent the night, and in the morning flew to New York and then on to Lackland Air Force Base (AFB), San Antonio, Texas.

We got to New York on a very cold night. The US Air Force had a bus for us for sightseeing although we got there around 10:00PM local time and a little late for looking around. New York was something that we could not comprehend. None of us spoke enough English or had any idea about the history of New York to appreciate it. The driver took us around the city and I was translating for the others. It was like the blind leading the blind. I didn't speak much English and to understand a New Yorker's accent was another issue. We spent the night in a hotel and in the morning flew to San Antonio via Braniff Airlines.

Lackland AFB was where all the foreign students went through a technical language school. We were taught aviation language. Of the group of 40 Afghan cadets, none of us had any familiarity with flying and had never been close to the cockpit of an airplane. Although all of us were to go through pilot training only 10 of us became pilots and only three of us became fighter pilots.

Language training at Lackland Air Force Base in San Antonio, Texas

The language school was for one year. We learned about the parts of an airplane, military aviation terminology, and everyday language. We went to class in the morning and to language lab in the afternoon. The whole experience was unreal. In this school there were students from all so called democratic countries who opposed the Soviet system of government. The school prepared us to go to another base where we joined the US students who were going through pilot training.

In order to get familiar to the American way of life and traditions, the school had a very good program where interested local residents of San Antonio came to language school and chose students to sponsor. The sponsors would come during the weekend and holidays and take us to their homes or to concerts or to a different town away from the city. They would cook American or Mexican food for us, and also take us to their church. I learned a lot of English from my sponsors, and also about the American culture and food. Even with all the conveniences of life in the US, we were very home sick. We could not call our families. There were no direct phone lines to Afghanistan, calls had to go through Paris, and then the operator there would call Kabul. At times we had to wait three or four nights waiting to get connections, but mostly it would fail, so writing was the only option.

Pilot Training School

This school was the hardest I ever attended. Almost all the students were young Air Force officers, many had private pilot licenses, some were navigators, and they all spoke perfect English. There were only a few foreign students; two from Iran, two from Pakistan and three from Afghanistan. We received our primary training in a twin engine jet (the T-37).

None of us had the slightest idea what we were doing, especially me. I could not understand the radio communication and got sick on the first day of my flight training. But we had to keep up at the same pace as our US classmates. Otherwise we would be washed out and sent backwards to another class. Or if the instructor pilot thought we were not pilot material then we would be sent to a course to become an aircraft mechanic.

The flying school had a program that was actually entertaining. For every dumb mistake we made the student paid a dollar. These dollars were kept until all students soloed out then the money was spent to buy kegs of beer and everybody celebrated. All the students should solo. The ones not able to were washed out. The day that you soloed you entered the class after flight with a cap that had the class logo. Out of about 70 students in the class 20 or so washed out and the only student remaining to solo was me. Every day for one week my instructor pilot took me for landings and when we come back, everyone looked whether I had my cap on, and would be disappointed when I still didn't have it. Not because they had sympathy for me, but because everyone wanted to party.

Once I soloed, I finished all of my training and flying hours faster than 95% of the students. It was a miracle for all of us to become pilots at the pace of the American students. The biggest obstacle was language. We heard different accents. My Iranian friend, who was the first black Iranian I ever met, was a great student but had difficulty with language. One day he was flying solo and ran into some kind of difficulty so he called the tower and explained to the instructor his problem. The mobile tower operator, who usually was one of our instructors, did not understand and asked, "Would you repeat your request? I did not understand." The Iranian student replies, "Sir would you repeat? I do not understand what don't understand means."

We finished primary flight training and were advanced to basic training in another jet aircraft. The F-80 was flown in the Korean war, but now was used as a trainer. It took another six months and I graduated from pilot training and became a rated pilot. All of this training was in Reese AFB in Lubbock Texas.

Life in Lubbock Texas was not what we expected. It wasn't like San Antonio where there was a downtown with many restaurants and bars and girls; it was very small town full of tumble weeds during dust storms, which Lubbock had frequently. On some long weekends Jamil and I drove to San Antonio to see our friends.

The students in our class were very close and extremely nice and cooperative with the foreign students. Most of the students were single and lived in barracks with us. One year of pilot training made us so close that we still keep in touch and celebrated our 45th reunion in 2008.

Reunion of Pilot Training School

In one phase of our flight training I had to fly a long, cross country flight. I chose to go to the Air Force training base, Williams AFB, in Phoenix Arizona. One of my Afghan friends was a student pilot there. I also met a Pakistani cadet who claimed to be a Pashtun from the Mohammadzai clan. I was curious to find out his family tree. At that time the Afghan government launched this concept of the Afghan land in the Pakistani side of the border and the Afghans called it Pashtunistan. When I asked this Pakistani cadet some questions I found out that he was one of my second cousins whose father never left the territory now called Pakistan. Unfortunately our countries were almost on the brink of war. When I came back to Kabul after pilot training, my cousin's sisters were in Kabul and one of the girls married a friend of mine and now they live in Germany.

Pilot training at Reese Air Force Base Lubbock, Texas in 1961

After graduation I was sent to Nellis AFB in Las Vegas, Nevada for advanced Gunnery school. I flew an F-86. I loved this aircraft; it was very maneuverable. We had instructors that flew in the Korean War and I learned dogfighting, air to air gunnery and bombing from them.

But before flying the F-86, every student had train on an F-80 with an instructor. This aircraft was a two-seater and once you graduated from that aircraft, you were able to fly the F-86 solo for the first time. Because this aircraft had only one seat, your instructor chased you with another and talked you through maneuvers.

I enjoyed flying over the Grand Canyon, that's where we would go for most of our training. I thought Las Vegas was a great city. We would go to casinos where the blackjack tables were for nickels, order free drinks and they would give us a coupon for the buffet which was one dollar.

To Lift a Mirror, for What You've Lost

We did gamble but I was smart and would play with only $10 dollars. If I lost... that was it. But if I won then I would continue for a while. My friend would play for a lot longer whether winning or losing and he lost a lot of his pay by the time we left Vegas.

After all this time in the United States I wanted to return home with the knowledge I had acquired, to teach my fellow Afghan pilots how to fly. And to tell them how progressive the Americans were and how we could change our country and make things better for the Afghan people. I was very patriotic and naïve and thought things could be changed easily with my very limited knowledge.

We could have asked for more schooling to extend our stay in the United States but I was so eager to get back home and change Afghanistan that I didn't listen to my other two friends. They kept telling me I was stupid and a dreamer that could not change things back home so easily. Nobody would listen to me and I did not listen to them.

CHAPTER SIX

My Return Home

Time to go Home (by Rumi)
Translated by Coleman Barks

Late and starting to rain
it's time to go home.
We've wandered long enough
in empty buildings.
I know it's tempting to stay
and meet those new people.
I know it's even more sensible
to spend the night here with them,
but I want to go home.

We've seen enough beautiful places
with signs on them saying
This is God's House. That's seeing the
grain like the ants do,
without the work of harvesting.
Let's leave grazing to cows and go
where we know what everyone really intends,
where we can walk around without clothes on.

In July of 1963, I finished school at Nellis AFB in Las Vegas, Nevada, and got ready to return home. My first stop was in Washington DC for a week. One of my childhood friends who went on the bicycle trip to Bamyan with me was in DC. I spent some time with him and while I was there I stopped and met the Afghan ambassador Mr. Maywandwal, who later was jailed by President Dawoud Khan for an alleged government takeover attempt.

Returning home, Kabul had not changed much, everything looked the same. I spent a week home and after that reported to the H.Q. and I was assigned to Bagram AFB flying a Mig-17 (a Soviet made fighter jet). When I returned my father was very proud of me. He would take me places and introduce me to people and proudly tell them what I studied in the United States.

One day he took me to Paghman to see former Prime Minister Dawoud Khan, who my father worked with for many years and was also my father's classmate when they were young. Mohammad Dawoud Khan was not in power anymore because of a disagreement on policies with the king. The king wanted to introduce a constitutional monarchy in Afghanistan and to present a new constitution. Dawoud Khan, who was an ambitious, patriotic and capable man, did not like the idea because he had other plans, which was one of the reasons he wanted to draft urbanites to the military; to establish his base of support.

When my father introduced me to him as a pilot, he assumed that I was a commercial pilot, but when he, out of politeness, asked me a few questions, I corrected him and said that I was an Air Force pilot. He got interested in me then and told me about his accomplishments. How he brought freedom to women without the consent of the king, and how this country needed young educated men like me. I was fresh out of school, and had been away from Afghanistan and its politics, so I didn't get that he was actually telling me a little of his objectives and plans for the future. I was so enthusiastic about being part of a movement that could bring positive changes for the country, I probably would have joined him, but not in a forceful or military way. I did not find about it until I was back in the United States. Being in the military in an absolute monarchy, away from society, and without the media, one can be isolated from what was going on in the background.

During the Cold War the United States and its allies were convinced that the Soviet Union was planning to introduce Communism to the whole world. The third world nations, especially the ones newly independent from the colonial powers, would be the first target towards expanding the communist philosophy; although according to communist theory, socialism should start in an industrial society where the workers are exploited by capitalists.

In the case of these third world nations, where industrialization is in the infant stages, the step toward industrialization could be skipped and Soviets could advance through national liberation movements to beat the capitalist nations and bring in a dictatorship to change the country to a socialist system. The United States and its allies wanted to contain the Soviet Union by establishing bases all around it through military alliances. In the Far East it was SEATO (Southeast Asia Treaty Organization.)

In Europe it was NATO (North Atlantic Treaty Organization) and in the Middle East it was CENTO (Central Treaty Organization.) The original name of this pact was the Bagdad Pact, but when Karim Kasim took over the country, he pulled Iraq out of the pact and declared it nonaligned. Iran and Pakistan were the neighbors of Afghanistan that were members of the CENTO pact. The United States trained the armed forces of both countries and provided them with modern military equipment. The regional balance of power was broken, and Afghanistan, who had territorial disputes with Pakistan, saw itself as a very inferior relative to Iran and Pakistan and, of course, to the Soviet Union.

Afghanistan wanted to purchase military equipment from the United States, but the answer from the US was negative. Vice President Nixon visited Afghanistan, and his perception was that this country did not have anything to offer the national security of the United States but left the door open by stating the US would provide modern weapons to the Afghan government free of charge on one condition: the Afghan government would join the CENTO pact. The Afghan government decided not to join for very obvious reasons. Afghanistan has a very long border with the Soviet Union and feared reprisal by the Soviets, and because Afghanistan was an active member of the nonaligned nations and had a policy of neutrality since World War I.

Actually this situation was not that much different from the great game of a century ago, where Great Britain wanted to stop the Russian Empire from reaching India. It established friendly governments around the Russians either by occupying them or, in the case of

Afghanistan, neutralizing the country by making it a buffer zone. This time it was the so called free world against the Soviet Union, where they wanted to encircle the Soviets and stop their advance.

History tells us that the Afghan kings in the past had tried to counter the threat of the British by approaching the Russians for help, but had been unsuccessful. The British government of India had successfully stopped the Russians short of Afghan borders by border demarcation and at times by giving some Afghan land to them.

After World War II, the colonial order of the world was starting to collapse. In the Middle East and Africa, many independent nations were emerging. In south central Asia, after India got its independence and Pakistan was partitioned, the Pashtuns on the other side of the Durand Line were not given the chance to decide their future by themselves but were annexed to this new nation of Pakistan. Afghanistan had a claim to the land which was separated from them by the Durand treaty. Now that India was a free nation and Pakistan created from the Indian subcontinent, the Afghans on the other side should have been given a chance to choose their own future but that did not happen.

Out of desperation, the government of Prime Minister Dawoud invited Khrushchev and Bulganin (prime minister and secretary of the Soviet central communist party) for a visit to Kabul and signed a treaty of friendship and non-aggression with the Soviet Union and brought up the question of an arms purchase from the Soviet Union. The Afghan government was very clever for doing this. The west and eastern blocs were competing in development projects with each other, and the Afghan government allied themselves with Soviets to create a balance against the Pakistanis who were allied with the west.

Nikita Khrushchev and Bulganin both came to Kabul and told the Afghan government that they would be more than glad, with no strings attached, to sell military equipment to Afghanistan. Of course that was not true.

The Soviets from then on trained thousands of Afghan military officers and many civilians in the Soviet Union, not only in their field of occupation but also in dialectical materialism.

I found out that my friends were right when they told me that I was a fool to come home. I sat on the ground without flying or doing anything except playing chess in the barracks.

My life at Bagram Air Base

I got to Bagram in July of 1963 and was assigned to the 2nd Fighter Squadron. I had to wait almost six months to get my first flight in a MiG-15 trainer. At the beginning I flew with a Russian pilot, named Kharkoff. After a few flights I was cleared to fly the MiG-17 the fastest fighter in the Afghan Air Force. After I got checked out, I became happier. I was chosen by the Russian instructor to fly with the acrobatic team in front of the king at an Independence Day parade.

Most of the flights were pattern, no instrument or night flying. Later on we practiced dive bombing and I was assigned to the acrobatic team with three other pilots. The leader was a short Pashtun from the south, trained in the Soviet Union. The two wing men were me and another American trained pilot. I lived in a barracks with six other pilots. There were bathroom facilities, water only two hours morning time, one hour lunch and one hour during the evening.

The base was in shambles, no repairs made. The commander of the base was living in the hospital, where I moved later, and then on to the public bath, which had unused rooms that we turned into accommodations. Because there were not enough rooms for everyone, we lived in any space we found.

We were allowed to go home on Thursday afternoon and return to base on Saturday morning. I commuted by commercial bus at first and later I bought a small Mini-Minor from a tourist; it was the only Mini in the country. It worked well for me; and at times that I wanted to sneak out of the base at night, the barrier by the gate was high enough for my car to go under. I would accelerate and paid no attention to the soldiers who yelled stop. I knew their guns did not have any ammo. When I returned I did the same. Pretty soon the soldiers knew me and would not make a big thing out of it. There was nothing to do inside the base especially during the winter time, when there was no flying for a few months.

A Mini-Minor

Most of the Afghans smoked hashish to overcome boredom. A couple of friends and I found a source of free alcohol. The MiG used 96 proof Russian alcohol for defrosting the windshield on high altitude flights. With the help of our mechanic friend we would siphon the alcohol out and mix it with watermelon juice.

I decided to rent a house outside of the base in Charikar, and encouraged a few friends to share the costs with me. I in return would provide the transportation back and forth. In Charikar we had the freedom to drink and party as late as we wanted. At times we invited our Russian advisors for a party. I bought the alcohol from a Hindu student of mine. I taught English to the 12th grade of Charikar high school and the girl school teachers without letting my superiors know. That's how I met the Hindu student; his father made moonshine called

Iraqee. When mixed with water it turned milky. So to get the booze without other town people seeing me, I would pass by my Hindu student's father's clothing material store and raise the appropriate number of fingers for the number of bottles I wanted. He would deliver the bottles to my house within an hour and give it to the soldier assigned to me as my servant.

Once a month when we got paid, all four of us would drive to Kabul to go to Bagh-e-Bala to eat and drink. Our favorite was steak and French fries and a bottle of military gin. We would spend half of our salary and foolishly drive back to Bagram that same night.

At the Royal Afghan Military Academy

August was a month where we got a lot of flying time to get ready for the Independence Day parade. The acrobatic group would start the day flying low over the parade grounds, then a steep climb out and some other maneuver. After the parade we would land back at Bagram and then were off duty for a few days.

To Lift a Mirror, for What You've Lost

Once a friend and I were in my Mini driving toward Kabul when a man appeared in front of us out of nowhere and I hit him. Since the car was so low, he smashed through the windshield. My friend and I were bloody with the broken glass and the man fell to one side. We immediately stopped the car to see how the man was, and started flagging the other cars to stop and help. Unfortunately nobody would stop. My car would start but had no power. The front hood was smashed to a point where we couldn't open it to see why. (Later, when the body shop opened it, they found out that a spark plug wire was broken and the car was going on only three cylinders.) I put the injured man in my car and drove about 40 kilometers to a hospital where some of my schoolmates were interns. Unfortunately the man died by the time we got there. I had to find the relatives and go to police station and tell them what had happened and to get my father involved since he was a judge in the court system. The police officers made it sound like I was at fault, guilty of killing the man. But this was changed to manslaughter and the punishment was 30 lashes with a whip and I gave a large amount of money to his family.

Life in Bagram became a prison for me. A future in the military was not what I wanted. I wanted to be something else, not a soldier. Maybe a commercial pilot or to go back to civilian school and become a doctor, engineer or anything but a soldier to protect the king and his family for the rest of my life. I would do anything not to be at Bagram. At one time I told my outfit that I was sick and to send me to the military hospital. I told the doctor that my throat was hurting and I wanted him to take my tonsils out. He checked them and said they really didn't have to come out, but if he did operate I would be hospitalized for a week. Sensing how I felt about returning to Bagram he offered that if I would translate the instructions for a new piece of equipment the Americans donated to the hospital he would give me three months rest. I accepted the offer and he took my tonsils out.

He operated on me in his office. A soldier who had absolutely no medical training or experience mixed the local liquid anesthesia in a bowl and injected it in my throat. They were cutting out my tonsils when the building lost power. The doctor couldn't see so he moved me outside in the sunlight and finished the operation. I was hospitalized for at least a week in a very substandard room. The surgeon told me, "Do not worry I will have someone to sleep in your room on the floor next to you, so if you have any problems he will help." There were no nurses on duty, but nothing happened and the nights passed without incident. The only person who visited me was my father. He didn't say anything, but wasn't happy to see me get operated on in a military hospital.

I translated the machine directions, got my three months break from duty, and didn't complain.

Bagram Air Base was built in late 1950s for the Afghan Air Force by the Soviets as part of the military assistance when the Afghan government started buying Soviet military aircraft and other war material. But after the Soviet invasion the base was strictly used by the Russians and after the US invasion now by the Americans for their own war efforts.

Bagram, similar to Guantanamo, is also used as a prison and interrogation center for captured insurgents. The base is located next to the ancient city of Bagram on more than 32 acres of ramp space and five aircraft dispersal areas, with a total of over 110 revetments.

Many support buildings and base housing built by the Soviet Armed Forces during their occupation were destroyed by years of fighting between various warring Afghan factions after the Soviets left. New barracks and office buildings are slowly being constructed at the present time. There is also a detention center which has been criticized in the past for its abusive treatment of prisoners. In May 2010, the International Committee of the Red Cross revealed that it was informed by US authorities about inmates of a second prison where detainees were held in isolation and without access to the International Red Cross usually guaranteed to all prisoners.

To Lift a Mirror, for What You've Lost

Soviet invasion era

Bagram Airfield played a key role during the Soviet war in Afghanistan from 1979 to 1989, serving as a base of operations for troops and supplies. Bagram was also the initial staging point for the invading Soviet forces at the beginning of the conflict, with elements of two Soviet Airborne Troop divisions being deployed there. Aircraft based at Bagram, including the 368th Assault Aviation Regiment flying Su-25s, provided close air support for Soviet and Afghan troops in the field. The 368th Assault Aviation Regiment was stationed at Bagram from October 1986 to November 1987. In 1987 a memorial was erected in honor of the five Soviet Air Force Su-25 "Frogfoot" pilots who had been killed during the war, including Captain Burak and Senior Lieutenants Aleshin, Zemlyakov, Paltusov and Hero of the Soviet Union Pavlyukov. The dilapidated memorial was discovered by US Air Force Sergeants David Keeley and Raymond Ross, and Army Sergeant Tom Clark in 2006. An attempt was made to preserve it as a historical site, refurbish and possibly relocate the memorial to the Russian embassy in Kabul, but it was ultimately destroyed by base personnel in 2008.

Some of the Soviet land forces based at Bagram included the 108th Motor Rifle Division and the 345th Independent Guards Airborne Regiment of the 105th Guards Airborne Division.

Civil War era

Following the withdrawal of the Soviet forces and the rise of the US armed and trained Mujahideen, Afghanistan plunged into civil war. Control of the base was contested from 1999 onward between the Northern Alliance and Taliban, often with each controlling territory on opposing ends of the base. Taliban forces were consistently within artillery and mortar range of the field, denying full possession of the strategic facility to the Northern Alliance. Press reports indicated that at times a Northern Alliance general was using the bombed-out control tower as an observation post and as a location to brief journalists, with his headquarters nearby.

Reports also indicated that Northern Alliance rocket attacks on Kabul had been staged from Bagram, possibly with Russian-made FROG-7 rockets.

US and allied forces invasion era

During the US-led invasion of Afghanistan the base was secured by a team from the British special force Special Boat Service. By early December 2001 troops from the 10th Mountain Division shared the base with Special Operations Command officers from MacDill Air Force Base in Florida and soldiers of the 82nd Airborne Division from Fort Bragg. The British force consisted of B and C Companies from 40 Commando Royal Marines. In mid-December 2001 more than 300 US troops, mainly with the 10th Mountain Division, were providing force protection at Bagram. The troops patrolled the base perimeter, guarded the front gate, and cleared the runway of explosive ordnance. In early January 2002 the number of 10th Mountain Division troops had grown to about 400 soldiers.

In late January 2002, there were somewhat over 4,000 US troops in Afghanistan, of which about 3,000 were at Kandahar airport, and about 500 were stationed at Bagram Airfield. The runway was repaired by US, Italian and Polish military personnel.

In mid-June 2002, Bagram Airfield was serving as home to more than 7,000 US and other armed services. Numerous tent areas house the troops based there, including one named Viper City.

By November 2003 B-huts, 18-by-36-foot structures made of plywood designed to hold eight troops,[8] were replacing the standard shelter option for troops. There were several hundred, with plans to build close to 800 of them. The plans were to have nearly 1,200 structures built by 2006, but completion of the project was expected much earlier; possibly by July 2004. The increased construction fell under US Central Command standards of temporary housing and allowed for the building of B-huts on base, not to show permanence, but to raise the standard for troops serving here. The wooden structures have no concrete foundation thus not considered permanent housing, just an upgrade from the tents, the only option Bagram personnel and troops had seen previously. The small homes offer troops protection from environmental conditions including wind, snow, sand and cold. During 2005, a USO facility was built and named after former pro football player and United States Army Ranger Pat Tillman.

By 2007 Bagram has become the size of a small town, with traffic jams and many commercial shops selling goods such as clothes to food. The base itself is situated high up in the mountains and sees temperatures drop to −20 °F (−29 °C). Due to the height and snow storms commercial aircraft have difficulty landing there, and older aircrafts often rely on very experienced crews in order to be able to land there.

On 18 October 2009 The State reported on Bagram's expansion. The article reported that Bagram was currently undergoing $200 million USD expansion projects, and called the Airfield a "boom town". According to the article: "Official US policy is not to create a permanent occupation force in Afghanistan. But it is clear from what's happening at Bagram Airfield - the Afghan end of the Charleston-to-Afghanistan lifeline - that the US military won't be packing up soon."

Bagram Airbase in the foothills of the Hindukosh

CHAPTER SEVEN
My Trip to the USSR

Returning to Bagram after three months, I heard that the Afghan government bought a squadron of MiG -21 fighters and one of our squadrons would be sent to USSR to get checked out in that aircraft. This was welcome news, because if I were selected I would have the experience of going to a communist country to see things for myself.

I was picked among the 30 pilots to go to Kyrgyz, USSR (currently named Kyrgyzstan) in the city of Frunze (currently called Bishkek) for training. After we got our passports at the Soviet embassy and bought a lot of things to sell in the Soviet Union, we flew on a Russian airplane and landed at Tashkent airport where they were supposed to have dinner ready for us. However, the authorities at the airport didn't receive any directions from Moscow and were not ready to feed about 30 or 40 people. So we were forced to fly directly to Logavoi and eat there, arriving at 1:00AM local time. At Tashkent, first we had to clear customs. Foreign goods, especially clothing like scarves, ballpoint pins, starched collar shirt, neck ties, and American cigarettes and so on could sell in Soviet black markets for ten times as much as what you paid for it. And our suitcases were full of items like that. The customs officers would want a cut or they would confiscate everything.

One Afghan officer ahead of me in line opened his suitcase and he had about 200 scarves, many ballpoint pens and shirts. The customs officer asked him that what was the purpose of having so many of those items—far too many for personal use. The officer replied they were gifts for his Russian friends. The explanation was not accepted and the argument started, escalating to the point of almost a fight. The Afghan officer who was wearing a Russian hat took it off and slammed it on the table as a protest and told the customs officer to go ahead and confiscate it all. The Russian was very happy to do that. When we left customs inspection, the Afghan seemed very happy. I asked him with the loss of so much stuff, why was he happy? He told me that he fooled the customs officer into not searching him, especially his hat. He had sewn about 100 old Russian Nicholi gold coins from the time of their monarchy that he could sell in Russia for a fortune. All I hid was $100 dollars in my cigarette pack and nobody noticed it.

The Afghans were treated very nicely. They referred to us as a society of peasants who were exploited by the feudal lords, and said that the Afghan people were hard workers and good neighbors who fought the colonialist British Empire for their independence and won with the help of the Soviets. What they were saying was impressive to me. I was searching for an ideology that could fit the circumstances of Afghanistan, start modernization, help the poor, get rid of old class structure and give all Afghans the same rights and opportunity. I wanted a society that would not treat the Hazara's and Shiites as second class citizens, and would bring equality among the people of Afghanistan.

My impression of the Soviets

While we were taught how to fly the MiG-21, we had a class in dialectical materialism and political geography and it was a prerequisite for all foreign officers. The ideology of Marx and Lenin was impressive to me and appeared scientific. I was interested in reading more about it and the Russians who had the duty of influencing us provided books in English for me and I brought them back to Afghanistan.

The masses of Soviets were purported to be equal; a doctor was not making much more than a janitor or a teacher. Everybody had a job and a place to live. It appeared all nationalities with the Soviet Union were equal, and the class struggle inside the Soviet states was dead.

While the utopian concept was inspiring, as I got to meet people and find out the truth, I became doubtful about the system. For example the majority of the Kyrgyz population was Muslim, but they could not practice their religion in the open. They would ask us to give them copies of the Koran since there were none found in the stores. The communist party members had more clout and power than the rest of the population, and corruption and drunkenness were common practice. The propaganda the Soviet's put out about the American society turned me off because it was not true. Their (the Soviets) caricature of black people handcuffed and being beaten by the police; the way it was portrayed was not true. The instructors talked about the class struggle in American society, and while the other officers who had not been to the US believed it, since I had been to the States before and did not see things like they described, to me it was meaningless and diluted their message. One of the instructors who knew that I was trained in the US came to me one day, took his hat off and asked me what I saw. I laughed and told him nothing but his head and hair. He asked again if I was sure, I said, yes. Then he told me that since I had spent time in the US I must have heard that Americans think that all Russians are devils and must have horns in their heads. Now that you see me, he said, "You know I am just a human being like anybody else, even though I am a communist."

The rooms and dining facility in Logavoya Air Force base were nice; especially when you compared it with Bagram. We had showers, a place to wash our clothes and enough food. We had assigned tables in the dining room and if we missed breakfast one day, next day our rations of eggs and bread would be sitting on our table for as many days as we missed breakfast.

Our ground school started before the flight classes, so we did not fly for a few weeks while learning the mechanics of the Mig-21. These classes were in Dari because most of us did not speak Russian. People from Tajikistan were our interpreters for class. The only other foreigners in the base were test pilots from India. From what we heard they were there to test fly a Sukhoi light fighter bomber.

My trip to Frunze

The airbase was in the village of Logavoya, a small village with a few houses, a grave yard and a train station. The only place for us to visit was the railroad station close to the base called Stance Logavoya, or Logavoya train station. To get to the station we had to walk through the graveyard which had the tomb stones of every denomination of Soviet society. The Muslim graves had the half moon, the Christians had the cross and the communists had the hammer and sickle. I kind of liked it, that all people were buried together rather than segregated.

The train station had only one place to eat with a very limited menu, but plenty of vodka. We visited that place a lot. The owner of the small store was Greek. I don't know how Greeks ended up in a central Asian republic of the Soviet Union, but he told me that he still considered himself Greek. The whole Greek community had applied to leave the Soviet Union many years ago, but the decision had not been made yet.

We had two days off during the weekend. The closest city was Frunze, the capital of Kyrgyz, a couple of hours away by train. Frunze was a large city with stores and restaurants, a university, parks and hospitals. It also had a military base, specifically to train military officers of developing nations. I met officers from many African nations. The main military hospital was in the Frunze airbase.

The first thing to do in the city was to find a person to sell the goods that you brought with you. You could go to a store, or sell it individually. The Afghans who were in the USSR before me knew a lot more than I. One of our friends knew the chief of police of Frunze and would take all of his stuff to him and sell it all for ten times the amount he bought it for. The chief of police would then sell all of it, especially the scarves, to Siberia and make more money. The Russians were dying to have western consumer goods, whatever it was. One of my friends would cut the label off his western neckties and then buy a cheap Russian tie and sew the western label on it and sell it back to the Russians and make a lot of money.

With the money we made from selling our goods, we lived like kings. The Russian girls loved us because we spent money on them. The restaurants loved us because we spent money and of course we loved it because we were in control.

There was one problem though.

When we came to Frunze we did not have a place to spend the night. You could not go to a hotel because you had to have a permit to stay. The proper thing to do was to take the train back to Logavoya, but some of us did not. We spent the night in the park with the girls we knew. All we needed was a blanket and sometimes a few couples got together and went to a girl's home if her parents were not there.

The town was alive after dark and hundreds of young people walked the city at night. Drinking was a big problem in the Soviet Union; you would always see several drunken people passed out on the street corners. When you went to a restaurant, the front door would be locked. A window would open when you knocked, then a face would show up. You either showed some rubles or a box of American cigarettes, then the door would open and you would be seated according to your donation. The food was soup and other Russian dishes. Almost all restaurants had alcohol. I did not see any mixed drinks in USSR. There was beer, champagne and of course vodka. You bought vodka by grams (a bottle would be 500 grams) and then ordered mineral water or lemonade on the side to chase it with.

After a few weeks of classes, we were ready to fly the MiG-21.

We first started with the trainer. My instructor was a Ukrainian captain. The first day we flew, he showed me the capability of the airplane by doing some acrobatic maneuvers like loops and Immelmans. Then let me feel the aircraft myself. He was surprised at my ability to execute the same maneuvers as he, correctly, and even better than him. He didn't know that I was in the Afghan Air Force aerobatic team and had trained with the US Air Force which was far superior to the Soviet Air Force. I was cleared to go solo in the MiG-21 interceptor version. I loved the airplane. It could go twice the speed of sound and I had not flown any American airplane comparable to this. The last US aircraft I had flown was the F-86, which was from the Korean war era and not as fast as this one. The training went very well and I flew to higher altitudes for training intercept missions and was

70

recognized for accomplishing the training better than the rest of the pilots.

A bad landing

One day coming back from a flight as I made my landing approach, I found that wind direction and speed had changed drastically from the time I took off. I was cleared for landing with a very high crosswind.

The MiG-21 had a drag chute in order to slow after touch down. You released the chute to slow the airplane, once slowed down then you ejected the chute and started applying the brakes. Landing in a crosswind with the drag chute was not easy because the wind blows the chute and changes the direction of your aircraft; you have to be very quick.

After the touchdown, I did not release the drag chute fast enough. The MiG started drifting to one side and left the paved runway. The night before it had rained and the sides of the runway were wet and muddy. The aircraft went into a ditch and bounced pulling about 8Gs then I hit the ground again. I shut the engine down, speed diminished and the aircraft came to a stop, but enough dirt went into the turbine and compressor that the MiG's engine was totaled.

Fire engines rushed to the site and a crash team got me out of the cockpit. I had no injuries and the accident was justifiably caused by conditions. I was warned the Russians punish their pilots for accidents, but that was not true. I was not punished. All I had to do was to write a report of the accident; maybe because they had hopes for me to one day help them invade my country.

Escaping from the hospital

During one flight at high altitude, I developed sinus trouble. I was sent to Frunze Hospital to be checked and was hospitalized for two weeks for observation. I felt fine after a few days, but they would not let me leave. I was bored, especially on weekends because everybody else was in the city. I made friends with an Azerbaijani Russian who was hospitalized as well and asked him to show me a way to get to town and see my friends. All I needed were some civilian clothes and a way to escape. He said no problem; loaned me his pants, shirt and shoes, and since he was on the first floor, promised to leave the window open for me. He said this was the way to leave after dinner, and come back the same way. I thanked him, gave him a pack of L&M cigarettes, and after dinner left the hospital and took the bus to town.

I went to the same street where I always met my friends and went to dinner. After eating, having a great time, I came out with a bottle of vodka in my hand. Suddenly I saw a young lady staring and waving at me as if very much surprised to see me. She was one of the nurses at the military hospital. Together we continued to enjoy a nice evening.

At about midnight, it was time to get on the last bus and return to the hospital. There I climbed through the ground floor window. The moment I landed, the lights were turned on and the Major on duty was standing right in front of me. I followed him to his office where he lectured me that if this incident was reported, they would send me back home. But he was going to be easy on me this time as he took the bottle of vodka that I still had in my hand. I found out next morning, he had drunk the whole bottle by himself.

The MiG-21 training was finished in six months. We did get a break in the middle when we all went back home and brought back to the USSR more things to sell.

I went back to Bagram air base and we started to fly the new MiG-21s the Afghan Air Force bought.

One day, the king of Afghanistan came to visit the base to see the new aircraft he'd purchased. He was accompanied by the Commander of the Air Force and Air Defense. The commander knew me and my family. All pilots stood by their airplanes as the king passed by. The commander and the king started coming toward my aircraft. The commander was saying something to the king. When he approached me, I saluted him and he extended his hand to shake mine and asked,

To Lift a Mirror, for What You've Lost

"Are you General Ghafar Khan's grandson?" I said yes sir and was surprised, how did he know? The king knew of my grandfather and complimented him. He asked me if I liked the new airplane and I responded with an affirmative, he wished me luck then walked back to his car.

CHAPTER EIGHT
After the USSR Trip (Finding Fahima)

Life in Bagram was the same as before. But one day I visited the H.Q. to see my friend who was the adjutant of the commander. The commander was just coming out of his office and saw me. He nicely invited me to have lunch with the rest of his staff, which I accepted. During lunch he asked many questions about my flying then asked me if I could translate a few books from the command and staff school that he attended in the US. I accepted the new task with honor. That way I could leave Bagram on Wednesday instead of Thursday telling the squadron commander that I had to see the big boss, which mostly I did not. I just wanted to leave and go to Kabul to my parent's house and see my civilian friends. Some were either still in college, especially the ones in medicine, and some of them were teaching in the engineering college run and funded by Americans. I went to the university to watch the girls, who were dressing very modern. I was looking to find someone to marry. My father and mother were also after me about that; saying it was time for me to get married. My father, who was truly an aristocrat who believed in tradition, wanted me to get married to someone from my own Mohammadzai clan. He would take me to all of our relatives' houses and show me their daughters.

I was totally against marrying a girl from my own family. I thought my family the privileged class that did not feel the pain of the people of Afghanistan. I was brought up with my friends from other ethnic and religious backgrounds and wanted to marry a girl from them. My father and mother never stopped me from pursuing my own wishes. At one point, I thought I was in love with a friend's sister from a wonderful, educated, Shiite family, and even sent my parents for her hand. Although the girl and some of the family members were in agreement, my friend for his own reasons did not agree with the proposal.

Life was very monotonous on base with nothing to do. The only time that I enjoyed being there was when we flew and that depended on many factors like availability of fuel and maintenance. I volunteered to take over a small canteen on base. A lieutenant, then in charge, had a total of about 3000 AFG capital in the market, and gave a lot of things to the base commander and other high ranking officers for free. I took control and would bring fresh fruits and dried fruits in my car. I did this in order to leave the base and be in Kabul at night. I even bought a refrigerator for the canteen, took over the whole bath where my room and office were and put in a ping pong table. Slowly the capital of the canteen went up. I would not give free merchandize to anyone, and while that made the commander and others unhappy, I was not scared. I knew pretty soon I would be leaving and going to the United States.

Finding Fahima

In Afghan tradition, young people get married not by dating like western boys and girls do, but by family arrangement. Of course the boy and girl should agree to it but romance and love comes later. When it comes to acceptance of any proposed arrangement, family name, status and the boy's education are very important. In Afghanistan at the time I was married the blessing of parents was very important. But the perception of arranged marriage in the west, as I understand it, means that the boy and/or girl are coerced into marriage. And that was not true among urban Afghans of that time. Unfortunately, now with conservative Islamic influence and that of non-Afghan Muslims, things have changed for the worse.

One day my younger brother, who was also keeping his eyes open to find a girl for me to marry, came to me and said, "Nangy, I found a beautiful girl for you. She usually goes to the Khyber restaurant with her family to dine, go one night and see if you like her."

I did go to see this girl and thought she was very pretty. She didn't even look at me; that made me like her even more. I was 25 and she was 17. I found out that her father and mother were my sister's friends and her grandfather was my father's classmate when they were young boys.

I sent my sister to her home to find out more about her, most importantly if she was ready for marriage. The answer was a big NO. Her focus on school, and she was still young were the reasons. So I put the idea on ice for the time being. A year passed and I saw her again while she was on her way to college. I looked at her, with such a desire that I had not felt for any other girl before. I knew this was the girl I wanted to marry. Again she didn't even look at me.

This time I sent my sister, mother, and some influential friends to ask her to at least meet me once. Her answer was still no, but I insisted and even sent my sister to spend the night at her house to find why she was refusing.

Her family liked the idea; having a good family name is very important in Afghan culture and because they knew everybody from my family, they kept on telling her "Nangy is a good guy, maybe she should consider meeting him." Finally she agreed to meet, of course with her family; mother, father, brothers, sisters, aunt and uncles all present. I had some experience dating girls when I was in the States and the Soviet Union and knew what I must do. I made her laugh all night and started talking about things we had in common like that we both enjoyed American movies. When I found out which actors or actresses she liked, I agreed with her even if I didn't like them. She told me later on that the way I shook hands with her made her and her sisters laugh. After a week or so my sister went to her home to find out what she thought of me.

Good news! Fahima told her parents that she would marry me. Her family was from Kabul and her maternal grandfather worked in the palace as the head of the department of written communication. He was a well-known literary scholar and a Sufi; well respected in the community. Fahima's paternal grandfather was probably the richest man in Kabul. He started his life by selling things on the streets when he was a young man. Totally illiterate, he built a business empire acquiring businesses and property. He even bought the royal palace, the former residence of King Amir Abdul Rahman where he entertained the royal family and the elite.

Fahima's mother went to high school inside the palace due to her father's connections. The family was very western oriented; the girls and boys wore western clothes and miniskirts, always the latest fashion. They all read western magazines. Fahima and her sisters never wore the burqa or traditional Afghan dresses. She and her sisters knew more about the Beatles and other western singers and music than I did.

Fahima's father became the head of the family at age 18 when his father died. He didn't have much experience in handling the huge businesses and property and mostly enjoyed life, his cars and trips abroad. When political parties became legal during the time when Shah Mahmood was prime minister, Fahima's father was a financial contributor to one of the anti-government newspapers. Due to unrest and demonstrations, Shah Mahmood resigned from the office and Mohammad Dawoud became the new prime minister. A new era of dictatorship began. Because of his anti-government contribution Fahima's father was taken to prison for a year and a half. He was beaten several times, and since the businesses and properties were without management the family lost almost all their wealth. One of their houses (the former royal palace mentioned above) was confiscated by the government and turned into a park. The family was not paid a fair price for it.

Our wedding

Our marriage ceremony was very simple and included only my parents, Fahima's grandparents and parents, an Imam, Fahima's brothers and sisters. I did not invite my brothers, especially my younger brother who was my friend and favorite, and I still regret it. The Islamic marriage was done, but actually (and practically) we were engaged.

Although we were married, by Islamic law, Fahima still lived with her parents and had not moved into our house yet. We were living separately but could see each other and go places together. Fahima loved movies but wanted to include the whole family, which I did not like but accepted. After a while my house was ready and now she could move in as my wife. We decided to have a big "going away" party instead of a wedding reception.

Our wedding

The party was in the beautiful newly renovated castle of Bagh-e-Bala, one of the palaces of Amir Abdul Rahman. We invited about two hundred guests and asked one of the favorite traditional Afghan singers of the time to provide entertainment. The party lasted till two in the morning. Fahima was going home with me that night. After we got home and every one left Fahima and I were going to go bed for the first time as husband and wife; she wanted to tell me something she had not before. I listened very carefully; Fahima wanted our marriage to be an honest one from the beginning. She told me she did not accept my proposals at first because she liked another young man.

Although I was shocked, and felt jealous of this other man, at the same time I was very proud of her honesty. The thought came to my mind that she might have been forced to marry me by her family even though she was in love with somebody else. I told her that I would not touch her or consummate the marriage; she was totally free to annul it because I would not be happy if I was the cause of sorrow in her life or any reason for hidden regrets. Fahima told me that I was her husband now, everything else was in the past and that she chose me out of free will and nobody made her marry me.

The rest of the time we spent in Kabul was nothing but parties and having a good time until the day came that we left our country for America. Unknown to both of us, it would be 40 years before we'd return.

CHAPTER NINE
My Second Trip to the US

The time has come... (by Rumi)
Translated by Nader Khalili

The time has come
to break all my promises
tear apart all chains
and cast away all advice

disassemble the heavens
link by link
and break at once
all lovers' ties
with the sword of death

put cotton inside
both my ears
and close them to
all words of wisdom

crash the door and
enter the chamber
where all sweet
things are hidden

how long can I
beg and bargain
for the things of this world
while love is waiting

how long before
I can rise beyond
how I am and
what I am

To Lift a Mirror, for What You've Lost

Back in Bagram I heard that the United States government had an invitation for a few Afghan Air Force officers, through their military assistance program (MAP), to attend a professional military school with the US Air Force. The Afghan Air Force presented 50 officers to the Ministry of Defense to be tested. If they passed the required test, then the defense ministry would make a selection of who would be sent to attend the school. I participated in the test from Bagram AFB; some officers were introduced from Headquarters and a few from the other bases as well.

The procedure was very strange. Nobody knew what the test was going to be or who was going to conduct the test. Nobody knew what to study and why the defense ministry was conducting the test rather than the Air force. The US Air Force had nothing to do with it. The only person who knew about the test material was an officer at Headquarters.

One Thursday afternoon, before this test was to be held, when I came home from Bagram, I was introduced to a very nice older man who was a clerk in my Father's court. He had some files for my father to look at on Friday, which was a day off for Afghans. While I was talking to him, he asked me if I knew his son-in-law who was also an Air Force officer, and had recently returned from the USSR. and was working at Headquarters as an interpreter for a Soviet advisor. I didn't know his son-in-law, but was interested to meet him since I was going to the Headquarters next Wednesday to see the commander.

I found him and was very surprised to find out the test that was going to be given to us was prepared by the advisor he worked with. I was extremely puzzled that the personnel to be selected to go to the United States must pass a test conducted by a Soviet advisor. I asked the officer what the test was going to be about. He answered that it covered leadership, tactics and other military topics... nothing about flying. I asked him if there were any material or references for me to get for study. He grinned and said that there was no material. The advisor teaches from his book for this course (which was for Majors and above); they take notes and that was it. If I wanted, he would be glad to come and study with me since he had been with this advisor for more than six months and had interpreted the same material over and over again

Lt. Kabir impressed me very much, and besides, I needed him. I thankfully accepted his offer and we went to lunch to get to know each other better. I asked him if I could do anything in return, and he said if I got to go to the US to bring him a 9mm hand gun if it's possible. At that time the restrictions on bringing weapons in luggage was not checked very closely. I brought a hand gun with me back home the first time from States. I told him I'd be glad to. For five days, Lt. Kabir moved into my room and studied with me for maybe 18 hours a day to cover three months of course work. I was so excited to go back to the States; I paid attention to every word and sentence as I absorbed the material. My brain was a camera and took pictures of all the information.

I went to the Ministry of Defense to take the exam. All 50 officers were present in a big hall, General Abdul Wali, the King's son-in-law and commander of Special Forces was also present. The test took about an hour and after it was over they wanted us to wait for the results, which would be announced later. That afternoon all the officers waited for the results. An Army captain entered the room and called my name and told me to follow him,

I followed him to another room where the general was sitting with a bunch of other high-ranking officers. I saluted and stood at attention. The general congratulated me, and wished me success, hoping that I would serve my country better with this opportunity of higher education. I thanked him and left the hall without going back to where the others waited. I was the only one who passed the examination. My grades were even higher than the officer who knew the questions. All thanks to my new friend.

I was selected to go to the US and attend the squadron officer's school which was located at Maxwell AFB in Montgomery, Alabama, and at the same time attend a few more schools to broaden my knowledge of the Air Force to apply them for the Afghan Air Force when I got back.

To Lift a Mirror, for What You've Lost

I had no idea how I was going to convince the Afghan Air Force that I had just gotten married and I wanted to take my wife with me. Nobody from the Afghan military was ever allowed to take any member of their family when they went abroad for training, unless they were a military attaché or very high-ranking officers. I would not settle for that.

I told Fahima and others that I was going to take her and there was no problem, they would understand my situation and feel sympathetic and would allow me to take my wife. At the same time I was scared to death of the consequences. I needed leverage.

I arranged to see the Air Force top commander, who liked me. I had translated his book for him, and I wanted to use my father's influence as well. My father told me that he saw the general at formal functions and they had a very nice and warm relationship, but my father didn't know the reason why. My father was the judge at the Court of Appeals at that time but the general's position was a lot higher than my fathers. My father agreed to go with me to meet the Air Force commander. We made a courtesy call to his house before breakfast, just to see him for a few minutes.

The general was extremely nice to my father. He invited us for breakfast and explained that he was a classmate of my uncle, who was older than my father. They both attended the military school together and though my uncle died at the very young age of 12, the general never forgot him. My father didn't know this. After he talked to my father about a few things, he asked the reason of our visit. I interrupted my father to tell him that I was just married, had been picked for this educational program with the US Air Force and I would like to take my wife with me to the States. He paused for a while and then said that this request was rarely asked since most of the officers were from the tribal areas and conservative Muslims; they would not take their wives abroad. He stated that he knew my family very well and he had no doubt about our love for our country, and I would be a great leader in the future. He also said jokingly that his gut feeling was that there was a possibility of me not returning, if I had my wife with me, but he was willing to take a chance. He told me to write an application and bring it to his office and he would sign it.

Call it luck, or God's work, or destiny; the application was signed. The Afghan government gave us passports. All I had to do was to go to the American embassy and get a visa for Fahima, which I thought to be the easiest task but proved to be the hardest. The military attaché didn't want me to take Fahima because he thought it would be very hard for me to study. Being a newlywed comes with a lot of responsibilities; finding living accommodations, spending time with the wife and entertaining her. She would have problems with language, loneliness and so on. It didn't make sense to me at the time, because my wife being away would be harder for me, but later on I found out that he did have many valid points. He won the argument and didn't give Fahima a visa, but promised to give her one after I finished a course at USC called Aerospace Safety and Management. I had to agree, but insisted that I would take Fahima out of Afghanistan and send her to stay with her brother for the duration of my course at USC if the kind sir would give her a letter for the American military attaché in Turkey to facilitate her visa to the United States after I finished the course. And he did.

Training in the United States at different bases and states

The course at USC was very challenging. There were officers from 15 different countries, my rank was the lowest as a First Lieutenant, and all others ranked from Captain to Lieutenant Colonel. It was a friendly group, they all had their accommodations and some were with their wives. I had no accommodations and nobody knew what arrangements the Afghan government made for me. One of the executives from an American company who was attending this course with us had rented a two bedroom apartment. When he found out that I had no place to live, he offered me a room temporarily at no cost until I found something. I accepted and moved in.

My salary from Afghanistan was only $90 dollars a month and the US Air Force was paying me $180 dollars a month. After I got my first pay check, I rented a room off the campus for $50 dollars a month. It was an old California bungalow in a very rough shape, but it was not too bad for that price. The remaining money after the rent was for other expenses, and I had to save as much money as possible until Fahima came. We could rent a better apartment when we traveled to other states.

When the courses at USC finished, Fahima was set to arrive in New York. I flew there to pick her up and we went to Chicago to attend another course; Jet Engine Accident Investigation.

I met Fahima at JFK airport. She was surprised to see me much thinner, I had lost about 30 lbs. She laughed at the clothes that I was wearing, a hippy necklace, bell-bottom pants and, according to her, a "weird" jacket. Fahima brought a letter to an Afghan girl who lived in New York and she had to hand deliver it. We had to take a taxi, which took forever and cost $9.50. I gave him $10.00; 50 cents for the tip. I was not familiar with tipping in New York. He was very mad and threw my 50 cents on the street and left.

The first time I had been in the States I spent money without much worry. I lived on base, the cost of the room was less than ten dollars a month, food was cheap and I was a bachelor. Now that I was married, I was so concerned with finances that I made Fahima angry when I was watching the cost of everything. I chose some of the worst hotels. She didn't understand that I had to support her with $270.00 a month for food, rentals and everything else.

After delivering the letter we took the bus to Chicago and from there to Chanute AFB, which was in Rantoul, Illinois. We stayed in a motel that cost $6.00 a night. Customs outside of the service (military) were absolutely foreign to me. Fahima didn't speak a word of English and had high expectations about being in America and the wife of a pilot. This made things difficult for us, especially for Fahima who left her family and friends and came to a foreign country with a new husband, who was still a stranger, and was thinking of nothing but studying.

The course was short, and soon we were on our way to Lubbock Texas for on the job training. I was happy to go because that was where I went to school for pilot training. I thought it would be cheaper to buy a car and drive. That way I would have a car and we would save on bus fare. I bought a 1960 Chevrolet for $190 dollars and we started our drive to my next assignment. I had spent time in the States before, but on a military base. Now with a wife who hardly knew me, I had to be everything to her and support her—while trying to figure out a lot of things for myself. Fahima spent her time watching TV that she didn't understand, couldn't go out or talk to people and waited for me to come home. At nights we had arguments, disagreements and even one time I thought of sending her back to Afghanistan. (Although the arguments continued, and at one point we even talked about ending our marriage, at the same time my love for her and her dedication and patience with me, gave both of us the courage to continue.) After all of these fights she would still fall asleep in my arms crying. One day we sat down and both decided to make our marriage work no matter what.

How could we disappoint our families, after they had become so close and were so proud of us?

When we got to Lubbock, we went to the base and borrowed some dishes for cooking. We thought it would be cheaper to cook at home. One day Fahima went shopping alone, she bought a can of tuna and was very happy that she found it at a very reasonable price. I had to disappoint her because the tuna was for cats. Since she couldn't read English, from looking at the picture on the label she thought the tuna was for everybody.

We rented an apartment for $120.00 a month and the people at the base were extremely nice. I even saw one of my former flight instructors who helped me get some flight time in T-38's, a new supersonic trainer. The liaison officer at the base found an Iranian couple at Texas Tech and introduced them to us so Fahima could socialize with them. We had a good time with our Iranian friends. They were students at the college and we would get together often until it was time for us to move. My next school was at another base in Texas; San Antonio, Randolph AFB. I took a couple of courses there which lasted about three months and when finished with them went to Maxwell AFB in Montgomery Alabama, for the school that I came to the US for primarily.

Maxwell AFB, which was also called the Air University, was a series of classes to prepare Air Force officers for leadership roles. The one I attended was called Squadron Officers School (SoS) and I have very good memories of this class. I was in the class (a group of 400 officers) with about 10 American officers. Most of my classmates were married and their wives were with them and they often invited Fahima to their homes. We were also invited to many functions inside the base where we met high-ranking officers and their wives. By now, Fahima spoke a little more English and understood it quite well.

A funny thing happened when Fahima was introduced to a southern lady as having come from Afghanistan. The southern lady I assume thought that she was from Africa. She got close to Fahima and touched her hair. She was very surprised that Fahima's hair looked and felt like her own; I think she thought that all people in Africa must be black and should have black skin and tight curly hair. Of course Afghanistan at that time was a relatively unknown country to much of the West; it happened to me on my first tour when I introduced myself to a pretty Texan girl as a guy from Afghanistan. She said, "That is wonderful, which part of Mexico is that?"

While at San Antonio we discovered that Fahima was pregnant. We had no idea what to expect and what to do. We had nobody from the family to educate us about what to do or not to do. If it were not for Dr. Spock and free healthcare at the base we would have been in deep trouble. We spent a lot of time in the hospital and asking questions.

I decided that Fahima should learn a trade and the easiest way was to send her to a cosmetology school because it didn't need much English. She would do practical work and that could keep her busy and when we returned home she could open a shop. Beauty salons in Kabul were very profitable at that time.

The apartment we rented was not very far from the base and her school but my classes started at 7.00AM and her school started at 9.00AM. So I would take her to town almost two hours early and she would sit in a coffee shop and wait until the school opened.

My school had two sponsors for me; civilian and military. They were the most wonderful people and I am still in touch with them. At times when I was away with the class, Fahima was invited to go stay with them until I came back. They invited us for dinner almost every weekend, and the ladies of my sponsors were a lot of help with Fahima during her pregnancy.

We lived in a house which was probably 100 years old. We rented the attic. Fahima was not happy during her pregnancy, she was sick all the time. One thing that she couldn't stand was the smell of the attic; it had this old smell of wood. So when I came back from school my first job was to wash the walls floors, kitchen and bathrooms with detergent to get the smell out.

Fahima spent a lot of time watching a TV that a classmate gave to us; it helped her learn English. After SoS was finished I had another course in Biloxi Mississippi; to learn how to be an Air Traffic Controller.

Hurricane Camille and Asya's birth

In Biloxi we rented an apartment by the beach which was not very far from the base. Fahima spent most of her time in the apartment. I got up at 4.30 in the morning went out and ran on the beach. At that time I was probably in the best shape of my life. I weighed 155 lbs., my high school weight. My classes started at 6.00AM, Fahima made a sandwich for me and then I was off to school. We didn't know anyone except a couple of young neighbors.

Fahima was very close to having the baby, and one day about 6.00PM she started labor. I took her to the hospital at the base and the doctor told me all we had to do was wait. He told me to go home and he would call when the baby was born.

I was truly a soldier and respected rank. He was a major. I saluted and left the hospital and went to the apartment. I told my neighbor that Fahima was going to have a baby, they brought beer, and we all got drunk. I was so uneducated in what I should have done. I was very trusting of the doctors and didn't know that I should have stayed with Fahima and been there to support her. On the contrary, I thought was I being logical; there was nothing I could do, the military would take care of her. The baby was born at 1.45AM or so. I got the call and went to the hospital half drunk. It was a girl and I wanted a boy. Fahima was fine, everything went well, and she and the baby were healthy. Fahima asked me where I was—why didn't I stay with her. I told her I'd been celebrating with the neighbors. She said she needed me because she couldn't understand what they were saying at times. After we came to California I learned that the husband was supposed to stay at the hospital and be with his wife. I didn't know any better at the time and regret my mistake. Fahima has not forgotten, but she has forgiven me.

Our little daughter, we named Asya, was so tiny. I couldn't wait to make her fat. (After about six months the doctor put her on a diet to not gain more weight.) Asya was a few days old when two important things happened. Armstrong landed on the moon, a tremendous boost in American morale in the Cold War with the Soviets, and Hurricane Camille hit Biloxi.

People were evacuating and I didn't know what to do until one of my classmates, Steve, called me and asked what I was going to do. I said nothing and he said I must leave our apartment near the beach and come to his which was located about ten miles inland and stay until the storm was over. I agreed and put Fahima and Asya in the car and headed to Steve's to ride the storm out with him and his family. Steve lived in an apartment surrounded by gigantic trees. After the storm we went out in the morning to look outside, the trees were on the ground but all fell parallel to the apartment. If they had fallen in the other direction, we all would have been killed or certainly badly injured.

We left Steve's apartment after two days and with difficulties traveled the 10 miles (it took us hours because of work on the roads and detours) to find out that the first floor of our apartment building was totally washed out. There was nothing left of it but the upper floor was intact. One neighbor who stayed upstairs during the storm told us the water, debris and washed out animals pounded the floor of his apartment. He said he saw death the whole night as if it was searching for him too. Our apartment was intact, but we had no water, power or gas. The Red Cross brought water and some food. We had to make a fire outside to wash Asya's diapers, and boil her milk bottles.

My training for air traffic controller was over and the next assignment was at Fort Walton Beach, Florida for a counterinsurgency class at Eglin AFB. The Air Force provided an apartment for us by the beach and we enjoyed the white sand and beautiful water every day. We stayed at this base for a few weeks and went to theaters on base a lot because it was very cheap, 25 cents per person. While in the theater one day, we heard some noise but nobody paid much attention. When we left the movie, we found out that a storm had blown the roof off of the theater.

Air Traffic Control School in Biloxi, Mississippi in 1969

After this school I was sent to Pope AFB, Fayetteville, North Carolina for more on the job training in the control tower. Asya was a few months old. I wanted Fahima to finish her Cosmetology class, so I decided to take the graveyard shift at the tower and babysit during the day. We had a military sponsor again, a very loving couple who often invited us to their home. The wife, Charlotte, spent time with Fahima. We rented a house in Fayetteville on an unpaved street (the first I had seen in the States). The house was heated with only one gas heater in one room. It was all I could afford. I took care of Asya during the day and most of my time seemed spent in the doctor's office; all these women with their kids, and me the only man in uniform.

Asya loved to watch TV upside down while she was setting on my lap with her head down and her legs on my stomach. One day I left her in her crib in front of the TV (I must have been preparing food or something). When I came back to the room, it was full of a horrible smell and the TV screen looked yellow. Asya had diarrhea and managed to spray it all the way to the TV.

* * *

One day a friend of mine from Fort Benning, Columbus, Georgia, wanted us to visit him. We found a place that would take extended/overnight care of kids for a few days. We left Asya with them for three days and went to see my friends. I was so trusting and didn't think it was wrong and truly there were many young children there. I made the decision to leave Asya with them but always had the feeling I was not right to do that and would not make that same decision today

Meeting the prince

Next stop on my schedule was Lackland AFB for another course. We put everything in the car, made a place for Asya in the back seat and started driving back to Texas. There we found a good apartment close to the base.

The first day of class, in the hallway I saw a young Second Lieutenant in an Afghan uniform. He looked at me but didn't salute and that made me very angry. When I asked another Afghan who this guy was, not respecting my rank, he responded that he was Prince Dawoud. That made me even madder. I said as a prince he should be an example and respect the higher rank. I was very idealistic and also anti-monarchy. The Afghan officer went and told the prince exactly what I said. That night there was a knock at the door of our apartment. It was the prince who came to apologize for what he did. He told me that he intentionally did that because of some high-ranking Afghan officers that came to kiss his hands and that embarrassed him in front of other foreign officers. He was a very charming and smart young man, always interested to talk about Afghanistan and the problems it faced, even at that time predicting that the monarchy was in danger. He stated that the royal family in the palace was always on the alert and close to their weapons. I am sure he knew more about the situation than I did. I had been away from home for two full years, and he had just arrived. The communist party was getting stronger, and Dawoud Khan was preparing to take over.

The day arrived that I should depart back to Afghanistan. Until then I had not said anything to Fahima about not wanting to return home. I went to the base travel office and told them not to buy my return airline tickets and that I would make my own travel arrangements. I told them I planned to fly to Germany, buy a car and travel home by car. They believed me and gave me cash for the expenses.

I had traveled to the United States as a student but the status of my passport was a service visa which did not have a time limit. When I decided that I was not going to return to Afghanistan, I visited the base legal officer and explained to him my intention. He advised me that I must not do anything while I was in training, and that I should get a social security number in order to work.

Two days later, my brother who I helped find a sponsor for him to come to the States to study, arrived in San Antonio. He told us that the situation was very bad back home. This was a reason to tell Fahima my plans. As I told her we would not return to Afghanistan, she cried that she would not see her family that she loved dearly. But said I was her husband and the decision was mine. Prince Dawoud came to say goodbye to us and put a wig on to make Asya laugh. When he left, Fahima said it was entirely their fault that I didn't believe in the system of government—and for that reason we'd never see our family and friends in Afghanistan again. She cried some more.

Breakdown near El Paso

In the morning we put everything we had with Asya and my brother in the back seat. We also took two gallons of oil, because my car burned oil. We left early in the morning without telling anybody where we were going; the destination Los Angeles, California.

We drove all day and night, stopping every few miles to add more oil to the engine. About 60 miles from El Paso, the engine stopped and apparently couldn't go another mile. There we were, in the middle of a desert, with no food or drink. I didn't know what to do and only had about $300.00 dollars in my pocket—all the money we had.

I decided to go to El Paso and buy another car and return to get my family. I hitchhiked and got a ride into town. I went to a used car lot and bought another Chevrolet for $200.00; the same kind that was broken down on the side of the road 60 miles outside of El Paso. I told the dealer that I kept my car in good shape, but since I didn't know much about cars, it could be a simple thing that I leave (give) that car to them if they would give me a ride and tow the car back to their lot. I told them my car was only a few miles away. They agreed.

The man who gave me the ride in the tow truck kept on asking how far to the car and I kept lying that it wasn't too far. We finally got to the car at about 10.00 in the morning. Asya started crying, she was hungry and we were in the middle of nowhere. Some people working on the highway passed by and brought some food and milk for Fahima, Asya, and my brother who didn't speak a word of English. When I got back to them, Fahima was in tears, saying if something happened to me, what would they have done?

The guy from the car lot fastened my old car to his tow truck and with Asya, Fahima and my brother in it; we rode all the way to the used car lot. It took us a few minutes to take all our belongings out of the old car and put it in the new one. The car lot man asked me what line of work I was in, and where I was going. I briefly told him my profession. He looked at me and probably thought, "Yeah right, you're a pilot".

The last thing he told me was to drive the car not faster than 30 or 40 miles per hour for the first 500 miles because they just changed the piston rings (or something like that). We stopped at grocery store and bought bread, milk, some fruit and other things and filled the tank. I thanked God that I didn't have to buy extra oil. We continued our journey to California. I had about 40 dollars or so left in my pocket and we had a long way to go to get to Los Angeles. But I kept going without panicking at the thought that I still had to rent an apartment, pay for food and so on. I was sure that I would find a job immediately. I could make enough to support us for a while until I found a job as a pilot.

At one roadside rest area, we stopped to have lunch. Soon another car stopped and a lady and a man got out of the car, sat down for just a few minutes, smoked and drank a Coke or something and maybe used the bathroom. Fahima was changing Asya's diapers and my brother and I were finishing the rest of some fried chicken (which I love). Fahima came out of the rest room with Asya and the couple had left. She saw something on their table and told me to see what it was. It was a small purse. I looked around to see if the couple was still nearby, (so I could let them know they forgot something) but there was no sign of them. Inside there was a pack of cigarettes, lipstick, and $100.00. I have to admit that I kept the $100.00. That $100.00 barely got us to Los Angeles.

We arrived in downtown L.A. found a cheap hotel room, and told the manager that I was looking for a job and needed his help. He looked at me and gave me a very kind look and said, "Go to Hollywood, a lot of refugees are there and plenty of work." I thanked him and headed there to look for an apartment. It took us all day, but we finally found an apartment on Hollywood Blvd. and we were very happy that we were going to live where the movie stars lived.

Finding a job in Hollywood

In the morning we went job hunting. Fahima was the first one to find a job, in a restaurant, the International House of Pancakes (IHOP), on the graveyard shift. After a few days I found a job in a parking lot. At first, for two or three weeks, until the owner found a parking lot for me to run, I was the person to go to each parking lot and clean them. In one parking lot there was a tree and the manager wanted me to cut it down. I was desperate for the job, said it was no problem and I would get it done the next day. The next morning they had an ax for me and I brought my flying gloves to wear. It took me all day to cut down the tree. My hands were full of blisters and the gloves were stuck to my hand. When I got home and took the gloves off, it was not a very pretty sight.

The manager of parking lot ("System's Parking Lots") liked me and soon gave me a good parking lot to manage behind the Famous Mossou and Frank restaurant, where all the movie stars came for lunch. They would tip well if you brought their car to them by the back door when they left the restaurant. Most of the movie stars looked at you like you didn't exist, but some were very nice. I met Ravi Shankar when he came out of the restaurant and of course I looked like him. He asked me where I was from originally, when I said from Afghanistan, he said, "Yes, I know Afghans are music lovers" and gave me a good tip.

Asya's accident

One night I was working very late and one of our neighbors (who was an Egyptian doctor, but worked in a hotel), came to me and said that my daughter pulled a pot of hot tea on her and was badly burned. She was in the children's hospital and Fahima needed me there.

I thanked him and said that I was responsible for all these cars and would not be able to leave until I returned all the keys to the car owners and closed the parking lot. It was the longest night of my life. When I left and went to the hospital, it was even worse to see my daughter, screaming in pain from burns on her face, chin and arm. It was terrible to have to do but we had to leave her alone in the hospital because we both had to work in the morning.

Another time Fahima called to tell me that Asya, who had been playing on the porch of our apartment, had eaten a can of Comet (the cleaning/scrubbing power) which was close to her. I was working that day with another guy, so I rushed home and took her to different hospitals, but they all refused us because we didn't have health insurance. From the Air Force I still had an ID card which had not expired so I drove to the nearest military (Navy) base. It took us a couple of hours to get there. When we arrived the doctor saw her playing and assured us that if she was still acting okay, chances were that she was just playing with the Comet and spilled not eaten it.

Finding an Afghan tenant

I worked at the parking lot and Fahima kept working the graveyard shift at IHOP and started back in cosmetology school to finish the required hours for the state. I had saved enough money to go to a flight school and get my flight instructors license. All this time we had no contact with any other Afghans.

The apartment building we were living in had only eight units. The apartment manager moved out and the owner told me if I took the job, he would cut my rent in half, which I accepted. One day Fahima was in the apartment, when an Afghan couple stopped by looking for an apartment to rent. They spoke Dari with each other, and Fahima was delighted. They moved in and we became great friends. He was the son of the then Afghan ambassador to the United States, and his wife came from our neighborhood in Kabul. She helped us with babysitting and Asya was very happy with them. They admitted later that when Asya refused to go to bed, they gave her a spoonful of wine and she slept with no problem. (I wonder why Asya still loves wine today.) Through them we met other Afghans as well.

A few weeks passed and I imagined that my friend Khalil told his father about our friendship. His father had a request from Kabul to look for an Afghan Air Force captain who had not returned home. The ambassador, who knew my father, called me and asked what should he answer? Should he tell them the truth? I asked him to tell them that he had not found me.

Dawoud Khan's presidency and my letter to my father

The bloodless takeover of government by Dawoud Khan was another drama in my life. My father knew that I had respect for him and considered him a very patriotic and modern thinking man. My father also knew that one of the main reasons I stayed in America was that I was forced to become a military officer and I didn't believe in the system of absolute monarchy. He wrote me that my opportunity was in Afghanistan and I should return to the country where I had an obligation to serve its people. I wrote back that I was ready to come back now, provided that my resignation was accepted from military. Even if I had to sweep the streets, I didn't mind, as long as I was out of the military.

I wrote a letter to the president stating that and my father decided to deliver it himself, since he worked with him when he was a prime minister and my father was a judge in the Court of Appeals. About two months later I got a letter from my father giving me his blessing to stay in America. Because the president was not the same person as before; he was surrounded by communists and had not allowed my father to see him.

The communists knew that taking over the country under a communist banner at the beginning would be almost impossible in Afghanistan, so they tried to side with a strong leader who was recognized and in power before. Once Dawoud Khan came to power, the communist party became very active recruiting members from the armed forces for their future takeover. My father perceived the future not to be bright, and didn't pursue the matter anymore.

If I returned, with the communist takeover, I would have the same fate as the rest of my Air Force colleagues who were trained in America. They were killed or put in prison under the worst conditions—though some of them did manage to escape.

One of my friends told me he paid a man to smuggle him and his family across the Pakistan border inside an empty fuel tank. At the border, his two year old son started crying. He said to protect the others; he clamped his hand over the mouth of his son for several minutes. He didn't realize that he was not able to breathe. His son survived by a miracle.

To Lift a Mirror, for What You've Lost

I found another friend in India and sponsored him and his family to immigrate to the States. He said when they put him in Pol-e-Charkhi prison, in the evening when the prison officers were drunk on vodka; they would bring prisoners to the courtyard while they stood on the balcony and shot them just like shooting at targets.

CHAPTER TEN
Working as a Flight Instructor & Real Estate Agent

I earned my flight instructor's license to be able to teach flying to students. I could now help them get their private, commercial, instrument, and multi-engine ratings; now I needed to find a position with a training school.

The Vietnam war was about to end and there were hundreds of pilots looking for jobs. That didn't make things easier for me. One day I took Fahima and Asya with me and traveled by car from L.A. to San Francisco, stopping at every small airport and submitting an application, For months there was no answer. One day I was working at the parking lot and as it was slow in the afternoon, I was reading the Los Angeles Times. I saw a one line classified ad: "Flight instructor needed at Aviation Associates, Brackett Airport, La Verne CA - apply in person." I wanted to grow wings and fly there right then before somebody else got the position.

I took the next day off and drove to La Verne, which was about 30 miles east of downtown L.A. The freeway was wide open, not a lot of traffic, unlike today where it takes you anywhere from one to two hours to get across town even during slow periods. In 35 minutes I was at the airport, where a man showed me the school which was located in a trailer.

I walked in and a fast talking man behind the counter asked me what he could do for me. I told him I was replying to the ad and wanted to apply for the job. He ignored my question and tried to sell me a membership in the flying club. I asked again about the job. He looked at me and probably saw desperation on my face and said he would test my ability as a flight instructor right then if I was ready. I nodded and he called a girl from the back office to come up and watch the counter.

To Lift a Mirror, for What You've Lost

We left the office and he led me to a nearby Cessna-150 so I could demonstrate that I was qualified.

Taking off he showed me the practice area and said to treat him as a student pilot, correcting all the mistakes he made. He had me demonstrate a lazy eight and some other maneuvers commercial pilots are required to know and execute. I did them and then let him do the same maneuvers as I commented and gave him guidance on how to perform them. After about an hour we returned to the airport. Once we were down he asked me how I would grade him if he were my student. I told him the truth. He needed to practice more, and with that, I thought he would improve. The man, Monte Testerman, shook my hand and said I was hired and could start any time I wanted. I told him I'd start in two weeks and returned to L.A. to give my notice to the manager at the parking lot.

I returned in two weeks and saw another man there who was the chief pilot. I said 'hello' and introduced myself. He responded with a grin, "You're the man my salesperson hired." Apparently Mike, the chief pilot, was in another state to pick up an airplane the school bought, and left Monte in charge until he returned. Monte later admitted that he needed a free lesson to learn those maneuvers and had started taking more lessons for his commercial pilot license. He liked me and had the authority to hire but not to test a new instructor pilot. Thankfully that did not pose a problem with Mike. Monte and I remained very close friends throughout my time at Aviation Associates and still are today.

Fahima and I quit our jobs in Hollywood and moved to a town next to Laverne called Claremont. We rented an apartment next to the freeway which was very noisy, but cheap and Fahima got a job as a hairdresser. We bought furniture and other furnishings on credit; I thought that because I was a flight instructor, I would be able to afford it. For the first month at our new jobs I made about $100.00 dollars and Fahima about twice as much. She didn't have any customers and I didn't have any students. I loved my job, but Fahima hated hers and went back to waiting tables.

101

In three months or so things picked up and I had several students, both new and those that no instructor wanted, either because they thought the students would kill them or the students were just not made to become a pilot. My philosophy was that I could teach a monkey how to fly; it just takes more time. The owner of the school loved me because being able to train more students brought in more money for him. My schedule got so busy that I even flew during lunch hour. After a while the chief pilot would block my lunch hour out so nobody could schedule me and write me a note... "Nangy, eat lunch please."

I loved flying and teaching. Since I had been an air force pilot who flew jets, people respected me and flying these small airplanes was not much of a challenge. I made a lot of friends, and since I was also an air traffic controller by training, all the local controllers knew me. My students were also very close to me, and invited Fahima and me for dinner and to join them to visit places. One Canadian couple became very close to us (I was the wife and husband's flight instructor) and we would spend a lot of time together.

As a flight instructor, even with all the flying I did and ground school, I still couldn't make enough money to be comfortable. Plus my job was in danger; I applied for a permanent residency through the US Labor Department and the school gave me a letter that they needed me. But every day would see a couple of US citizens apply for jobs who were qualified pilots and Vietnam veterans, but the school would find an excuse not to hire them. Because of this I didn't see a future for me at this business either. I was working long hours, on commission. If the weather was bad everyone cancelled their flights and I made no money. I started searching for other opportunities. I decided to go to real estate school and became a real estate agent. I went to school, took and passed my test and was ready to start at my new profession.

My real estate career

An Afghan friend of mine who a year ago was working in a mental institution hardly making ends meet visited me one day. He drove up in a Rolls Royce with his beautiful girl friend and invited us to his apartment in Marina Del Ray. My friend now worked for a large company that was selling land in the desert to people. My friend was an excellent salesman and managed to sell quite a few parcels to people and impressed the management with his abilities. He became a manager of the sales department in a very short time. He said he would give me a job tomorrow as a real estate agent since I had a license. I was very excited and agreed to go to his office.

***

The next day I went to Beverly Hills and climbed I don't remember how many levels to reach the office. I was introduced to a man, an Iranian-American, with a huge diamond ring on his finger; he immediately took me to the class. The class started and I began to learn (as they explained it) the property that we were going to sell was in the desert... but it was a bargain for real estate buyers (according to them). The following day we all went on a bus to tour this property in the Lancaster area. The town looked good, though I didn't see the lake or golf course. Still I was quite satisfied that the property in this town could be sold. When we returned to the office, the instructor said if we wanted to be rich like him and other people who worked with him, the first rule was that we had to buy a piece of this land and sell parcels to our closest friends and family.

That was not the only disconcerting issue about this "opportunity". I found out that the land we were to sell was not even close to the town they showed us. It was located in the middle of the desert far away from everything. A lot of people were fooled and bought that land. I couldn't do that to my close friends and family, so that was the end of my real estate career. My wife tells me I am the most restless person she knows, she is right, I am always looking for challenges. When real estate did not work out then I took to a bartender's class and got a license for that but that did not work out either. The real state school did end up helping me when it came to looking at listings for restaurants.

* * *

All of our friends were this circle of pilots and air traffic controllers so all we talked about were flying and airplanes. We knew a few Afghans who lived in Hollywood or in San Fernando Valley, but we did not see them much. Fahima was still working at IHOP as a waitress and she got close to this wonderful lady (Veda) who was her coworker. We became very close friends. One day she invited us to her home for dinner. She had three beautiful red-haired children who probably had never associated with foreign looking people like us. When we knocked on the door and the kids answered they ran to their mother and announced that the brown people are at the door.

Veda, I assume like many other Americans did have some knowledge about other faiths but kind of mixed them all up. Probably Hollywood movies had some influence on her thoughts. One day she came to our apartment and was surprised not to see the idol we worshiped at the entrance. She wanted an explanation about that but never showed any disrespect to us and she still remains one of dear friends.

Another friend that we associated with was a girl who worked with me in flight school as a secretary. Her name was Candy. Being a foreign born and not accustomed to American names, I had a hard time remembering names; and sometimes got confused. But I could associate Candy with something sweet and often called her Sugar. (This was funny to her but very funny to Fahima that I would call another woman Sugar.)

Candy came to our apartment one night with her boyfriend who was a Swiss; a hippie with long hair and beard. We cooked Afghan food for them, and he had a gift for me. After dinner he took a bag of marijuana out of his pocket and rolled a cigarette with it and offered it to me to smoke. This might be very difficult for Americans to understand, but my Afghan blood still flows in my veins and I could not say no to my guest, and I smoked with him. This was the first time in my life that I smoked grass. I come from a country where hashish was in abundance but I never got even close to it.

To Lift a Mirror, for What You've Lost

We would spend most of our weekends flying to airports nearby. Asya loved flying and Fahima never panicked or was scared of flying. Of all of those weekends flying, one of them was especially memorable. It was our anniversary and I decided to take Fahima to Catalina (an island about 30 miles offshore from Los Angeles.

The island is privately owned by the Wrigley family (who make chewing gum). It has a runway right on top of the mountain with cliffs on both sides. Next to the runway there was a beautiful restaurant where you could see the ocean on either side with wild buffaloes grazing around the island. We took off with partly cloudy skies and by the time I got to Catalina it was totally overcast over the island. I was disappointed and did not want to turn back, but I found a hole in the overcast and could see the runway with plenty of clearance from the clouds. I circled and got below the clouds and landed. It was pouring rain and we managed to park close to the restaurant and get inside. The fire place was on, we were the only two customers and watching the rain hit the windows and the wild buffaloes outside; just Fahima and I alone, made it the most memorable anniversary.

CHAPTER ELEVEN
Buying the Restaurant

Wonder (by Rumi)
Translated by Coleman Barks

God picks up the reed-flute world and blows.
Each note is a need coming through one of us,
a passion, a longing-pain.
Remember the lips
where the wind-breath originated,
and let your note be clear.
Don't try to end it.
Be your note.
I'll show you how it's enough.
Go up on the roof at night
in this city of the soul.
Let *everyone* climb on their roofs
and sing their notes!
Sing loud!

Not satisfied with the jobs I found working for someone else; I always looked at the L.A. Time's business opportunity section and especially at the restaurants for sale. I thought of opening an Afghan restaurant somewhere close to my work and having Fahima run it. I could help if she needed me.

I started looking for small restaurants everywhere in the area. We even went all the way to Long Beach looking for restaurants. I would go for anything, but Fahima would look at it, consider it and disagree. If it were not for her I would have bought the worst restaurant ever—just because the owner accepted what I could offer. One day an ad about a small coffee shop in Claremont caught my eye and I thought, 'It won't hurt to just go look at it.'

To Lift a Mirror, for What You've Lost

I went and had lunch. The place was very small, about 35 seats, closed on Sundays and business hours from 5.00AM till 5.00PM. The kitchen was inside the dining room, and if you wanted to go to the restroom, you had to go through the kitchen. I thought, 'for a start it would do.' The asking price was $24,000.00 and the owner would take $8,000.00 down and the rest could be paid monthly for five years. This all seemed reasonable and a very good deal. I had a problem though. I didn't have enough money for the down payment so I kept looking for something I could afford and forgot about that restaurant.

After a few months, one day I saw in the paper the same ad—the restaurant was still for sale. That night we were at one of my student pilot's home for dinner, and I mentioned the restaurant. My student, who was a very successful plumber, asked, "Why don't you buy it?"

I replied I only had $4,000 dollars saved and the owner was asking $8,000 down; I couldn't afford it. He looked at his wife and they said, "Nangy, if you really want to buy the restaurant, I will loan you the money."

I didn't know how to thank them. I said that if they were serious, I would accept the loan, but I wanted them to be my partners. They agreed to that but only as an investment; they didn't want to get involved with operating a restaurant. That was a perfect arrangement for me and Fahima. Except that when we took over the restaurant; we didn't have any idea how to run one. The only person who knew a little was Fahima, from her waitressing experience. I didn't know anything about cooking but the kitchen was the logical place for me. So that's where I started.

We kept the name, *Walter's*, but changed a perfectly good menu and let workers for the previous owner go. The first day or so everybody came to see who these new people were with strange food ideas. One person asked me if the Afghan burger was made with Afghan hound's meat. We obviously didn't know anything, and after a couple of very busy days, we lost almost every customer that coffee shop had. Thankfully, a few college students and their professors became very good friends with us and besides giving us business; they educated us in what to serve. We had to learn fast. One thing that scared Fahima about owning restaurant was that we both would live the rest of our lives in it. We would not be able to have a life outside that restaurant and see our friends, which at this time were quite a few Afghans. I told her we would get better and bigger and someday would have a large staff and we would only manage the business.

We opened the restaurant at 5.00AM just for four customers who spent about $1.00 each, but were scared to lose even that little bit of money. Fahima opened the restaurant and I came at 8.00AM after taking Asya to a Christian kindergarten. Fahima went home at 2.00PM to pick up Asya and would come back to the restaurant to eat and I stayed till 9.00PM to close. Fahima helped me clean the kitchen while Asya played hide and seek with one of our wonderful customers (one who stayed loyal and remained a customer after we began running the restaurant). They helped us with babysitting Asya and were teaching her to play piano (though she actually played hide and seek and other games more than playing the piano).

The business didn't get better; we managed to stay open, but I thought that we were going broke—a day at a time. At this critical time, another beautiful restaurant opened nearby with great ideas and a menu of fresh sandwiches. The new restaurant included a patio for customers to eat outside. People waited an hour to get a seat and all other restaurants in the village, which were only a few, didn't have many customers.

Determined to do something to change things I started remodeling the restaurant. Another of my pilot students, who was a carpenter, would come to help me. We would work till late hours of the night, and he never asked for any money in return. The remodeling, opening a small outside eating area, and serving a few well-prepared Afghan dishes slowly helped bring in more customers. In the meantime we learned a lot from the newly opened restaurant; even Fahima would venture to that restaurant after we closed at 5.00PM and come back complimenting their dishes to me. I was jealous to hear that, but we would copy their dishes with a little twist to make our own.

One thing which helped the restaurant was that the residents of town and the students and faculty of the local colleges were very interested in my background as a pilot, a flight instructor and being from Afghanistan. So many people who were pilots and found out that I flew jets, especially Soviet jets, would come to the restaurant. Besides eating they would visit with me for hours and would bring more friends.

In the village most of the few restaurants and businesses didn't stay open late. If people were going to eat out they didn't come to the village because there were no worthwhile restaurants there to impress people. And none of the restaurants were open on Sundays. I decided to do both. I opened the restaurant for breakfast on Sundays and stayed open in the evening till 8.00PM. The Sunday breakfast was a success right away. The dinner was not, but I insisted on staying open.

Another project I had was to get a beer and wine license and rent the space next to the restaurant to create a patio bar. I went to the landlord's office for the first time and asked him about buying a license for beer and wine. He had his doubts about the patio, but he gave his blessing. Now I had to get a permit from the city. Claremont was very conservative. They didn't want expansion of the village and always resisted change. They allowed me to have the patio, but I had to pay a fee that came to thousands of dollars. If it were not for Herb Hafif the building owner, I wouldn't have been able to pay for it.

The outside patio was opened and slowly we built some business. The capacity of the restaurant increased from 45 to about 100. Winter came and the small coffee shop couldn't handle the extra customers. The inside of the coffee shop had a capacity of only around 30-40 people. We then rented an adjacent bungalow that was vacant and turned it into another dining room

I hired a beautiful young girl as a hostess and found out that she and her parents emigrated from Russia recently to America. Her father was a movie producer in Leningrad and knew a lot of the officials of the post-communist era. One day while I was taking a little break at home, her father knocked on the door and wanted to speak to me. He had a can of wonderful Russian caviar as a gift for me, and stated that he had access to a castle in Leningrad (St. Petersburg) and could get that for me to make it into a restaurant. He was impressed with *Walter's* and wanted to be my partner. I thanked him but didn't accept the offer.

I met her parents again in my friend's house one night. When somebody asked her mother about the Afghan war with the Soviets, she stated that the Afghans were like barbarians, that was why the Soviets had so many problems with the war. I became very mad and took it personally. I told her let's compare: the Russians bomb villages, killing women, children, and men indiscriminately. They destroy their farms and homes and water reservoirs. Above all, the Russians had invaded the home of Afghans, while Afghans in their own primitive way were fighting for their way of life against one of the largest most sophisticated armies of the world.

I asked her, *"Which one do you think is the barbarian?"*

CHAPTER TWELVE
Meeting the Hafif's and
Corporate Flying

The original coffee shop was located next to some California bungalow style cottages which had six units. These bungalows were owned by Herbert Hafif (our landlord), and were in very bad shape. They were occupied by old people who couldn't afford housing anywhere else. This was a good thing for me, because every time a renter moved or died, I rented that bungalow and converted it to a dining room. It wasn't a grand design, but it gave the restaurant a unique look that nobody else could copy. I even dug under the cottages and made a wine cellar and bakery under the bungalows while the dining rooms on top were open for business. It took me two years, digging one bucket of dirt at a time. I did a lot of this digging without a permit, and once done, then got the permit. (Herb would joke with me and say, "An Afghan is always an Afghan. They dig tunnels." Except in Afghanistan they dig tunnels in the mountains to use as staging points to surprise and attack their enemies. You do it in Claremont to surprise city hall.)

After I got to know the Hafif family better, and flew them around as their pilot, we became good friends. Herb's wife Kay was a very good chef who took a lot of courses in Los Angeles with many celebrity chefs. She came to *Walter's* one day and shared one of her recipes with Fahima. I still remember it was babyback ribs. We prepared the recipe and invited Herb and Kay for dinner that night. At the end of the dinner, I asked Herb how he liked the ribs. He was honest and said that it was the worst ribs he ever had. Fahima and I were so disappointed we didn't know what to say. The night passed and a few days later Kay, who felt very bad for what Herb said, invited Fahima to go to Los Angeles with her for lunch, just to apologize for Herb's behavior. This lunch actually changed our way of cooking and the future of *Walter's*. Fahima went to Paris with Kay (although I couldn't afford it). She took cooking and baking classes in Paris and later for two years took classes in *Ma cuisine* in Los Angeles and other cooking schools and started introducing new recipes at *Walter's*. We both became foodies and followed the celebrity chefs and even became members of the California Food and Wine Institute. I got interested in learning how to cook and took some of the courses with Fahima.

I remember one day I was in the back kitchen preparing something, when Fahima came to me very upset. A customer who was very offensive didn't want to pay for what he ate. Fahima wanted me to come and defend her. I said, "Don't worry, I will handle him." I went to the front to talk to this rude person. I planned to tell him his behavior was unacceptable and was not the way to talk to a lady and that he should pay his bill and leave. When Fahima showed me the man, there was no way I was going to tell him anything; he was about 6 feet 8 inches tall and very strong looking. Instead of getting mad, I started to say hello and so on, to try and make small talk instead. The man left the restaurant without saying a word or paying but I was very happy. I told Fahima to choose a smaller guy next time she gets into a fight. That guy could have killed me if I had said anything he didn't like.

Herb Hafif was, at that time, a well-known trial lawyer and at one time ran for the governor of California and asked me if I could fly him around California during the campaign. I agreed, but had to refuse a lot of flights due to my work at the restaurant. I didn't let flying get away from me even though I was working full time at *Walter's*; I still had students. The flying school I started with still had a lot of respect for me and kept me on their staff with the full privileges of a flight instructor.

When Jimmy Carter ran for the president of the United States, he chose Herb to be his campaign co-chairman for California. I had the privilege of flying Mrs. Rosalyn Carter one day to Santa Barbara, where she was giving a fund raising speech. We picked up Mrs. Carter in Burbank and flew to Santa Barbara, where we were picked up by supporters of the Democratic Party and went to this beautiful seaside resort, where a lot of rich people were gathered.

To Lift a Mirror, for What You've Lost

After the speech, Mrs. Carter received a call from Washington (or her husband) to fly back from Santa Barbara, not from Burbank as was planned. The rest of us, Herb Hafif, some reporters and the Secret Service detail were flying back to Burbank. It was getting dark and clouds were building. I had to file an IFR flight plan to get out of the airport and fly IFR (on instruments due to the poor visibility) all the way home. Everything went well until we got to San Fernando Valley, over the Van Nuys outer marker. I heard a very loud noise and all of a sudden the right portion of the front windshield went dark. I looked at the gauges and saw the right engine had lost all RPM and immediately shut it down. I knew my location and that Van Nuys airport was right under me because I had taken many students for practice there. I declared an emergency and asked permission to land. I broke out of the clouds and the passengers started panicking and asking questions. Herb who was sitting in the back seat told them to quiet down and leave everything to the pilot. He even joked that the Republicans must have known we are coming and shot us. I landed the airplane safely without an incident, but couldn't taxi with one engine (because it would go in circles). They had to tow the airplane from the runway. The airplane was fixed (after replacing the engine and broken propeller) and I flew it back to Cable airport where it had a hanger.

I flew that same airplane to Lake Havasu a few times and after the last trip, returning really late, I parked the airplane and came home. In the morning I went back to pick up my jacket and refuel the airplane, but the airplane wasn't there. I called Herb and told him about it. The airplane was missing for almost two months. One day, at the restaurant, I was visited by two federal agents that asked me a few questions. After they were satisfied with my answers they told me the airplane had been found, and anytime I was ready I could go to where it was and fly it back to Claremont.

The airplane had been stolen by a pilot who was living in our neighborhood; knew where I lived and approximately when I flew the airplane. He stole the airplane, flew it to Mexico, took all the passenger seats and co-pilot seat out, and filled the airplane with marijuana.

During the night, probably under the radar coverage, he flew it back to the US. When he got close to his destination, he got tired and landed in an uncontrolled airport in Kingman, Arizona (an uncontrolled airport does not have anyone in the tower at certain times—typically nighttime). He parked the airplane and pulled the shades and went to a motel to spend the rest of the night. The airport manager showed up in the morning and found this unknown airplane with the curtains closed. Out of curiosity he went over to see why the shades were closed and smelled something funny. When he looked inside, he knew what was going on and immediately called the DEA. When the pilot showed up to leave, the DEA agents arrested him. The reason the agents asked me questions was they had their doubts whether I had something to do with it. *'Being an Afghan-American and coming from the land of plenty (so to speak).'* I flew to Kingman in a day or so, had to air out the cabin for a few hours, dump the fuel out of the airplane (because he filled it with wrong fuel) and then flew back to Cable airport to begin repairing the airplane.

* * *

When I was back in Afghanistan, after graduating from high school, all of my friends got to go to the college of their choice except me. I always felt like I was cheated out of the education I wanted although things turned out okay. I did go abroad before all of my friends and even went to the Soviet Union. But I always wanted to go back to college for higher education. With the restaurant doing well and able to also continue my flying career, I decided to go to graduate school.

I stopped at Claremont graduate school and talked to the Dean of International Relations department, Professor Neal, who became my good friend. I explained the schooling and experiences I had and he told me that he would talk to the admissions office. In a week or so when I checked back, he said that based on my education and experience, he would allow me to enter the PhD program on one condition: that none of my grades go lower than B+. That was great news to me. I entered the program and my grades never went below B+. I was going back to school not to change careers, but to satisfy myself academically. Of course I knew it wasn't going to be easy. I was teaching flying, flying as a corporate pilot, running a restaurant, raising two kids and now going back to school, but somehow I managed.

We lived in a house about two miles from the restaurant. We bought the house in 1975 and Dawoud, my son, was born there. We had great neighbors and it was in a good neighborhood. One night in 1987, about 2.00AM, we got a call from the Claremont police department that *Walter's* was on fire and they wanted me to come there as soon as possible. Fahima and I got up and rushed to the restaurant. From a mile back we saw the flames burning the whole building. It was a mess. The beautiful stained glass which was made by a famous Claremont artist, Mike Hill, and the woodwork inside the restaurant was either burned or destroyed by the fire department. The cook who was working the last shift drank a few beers and forgot to turn off the burners in the kitchen, but shut the exhaust system down. The heat built up and had no way to escape but out through the dining room burning through the woodwork.

The kitchen had a strange exhaust system; the grease had built inside it for years and there was no way to clean it—the fire in a way solved that but took the building with it. All the pests in the attic were taken care by the fire along with the grease buildup. Fahima and I thought that this was the end of our restaurant career. We didn't have enough insurance coverage. How were we going to live and rebuild the restaurant? We didn't have any answers to that at first.

In the morning we dismissed all the workers and closed the restaurant, to figure out how to rebuild. The first order of the day was to remove the debris. We started a few days after the fire. All of my kitchen crew came back and told me they would work without pay until all the debris was cleared off. As we were moving the debris day after day; our neighbors and customers provided lunch for the whole crew every day, and the landlord, Herb, promised to help us with the rebuilding costs not covered by insurance coverage. With the help of our friends and customers we built a new restaurant with separate bathrooms and kitchen. Walter's Coffee Shop became *Walter's,* the restaurant.

Walter's restaurant became a popular place for meeting and seeing people. Professors brought their guests and town's people who were my customers for years gave us a lot of support and business. The number of customers kept growing and we were the most popular restaurant in town. We even got ahead of that famous restaurant that pioneered outdoor dining in Claremont. I was anxious to expand, to create more dining space, so I rented more bungalows. I had five of the six bungalows, plus the entire patio. Of course I did the additions one year at a time. When the students and faculty came back from vacation there was always something new at *Walter's*. It was great for business, but not so good for my pocket book. I invested every penny I made back into the restaurant; hired more people, added more space, and totally remodeled the kitchen with new equipment. We expanded to accommodate weddings and charity events and my staff went from a total of six employees including Fahima and myself, to nearly 100 and the restaurant capacity increased from 40 or so to 400.

CHAPTER THIRTEEN
The Russian Invasion of Afghanistan

Mohammad Dawoud Khan was a dictator that ruled with an iron hand; his intelligence service was very powerful. He was brought to power after the Prime Minister Shah Mahmud, the king's uncle, failed to control the opposition when the king wanted to bring in a constitutional monarchy and new constitution.

Dawoud Khan accomplished a lot for the country with his first round of leadership; the most important of his accomplishments were freedom for women who did not want to wear a burqa, an improved role for women in Afghan society, infrastructure projects, a policy of neutrality and modernizing the military. His policy was to allow both the Russians and Americans to compete in development projects in Afghanistan. Afghanistan was denied by America to buy weapons, but the Russians did sell weapons to Afghanistan.

In 1978, President Dawoud and his family were assassinated and the communists took over the government of Afghanistan. The officer who ordered the bombing of the palace and the murder of President Dawoud was in my squadron. Most of my friends who studied with me in the United States were either killed or put in prison. I would have been killed for two reasons: I was educated in the United States and I was a Mohammadzai, the tribe of the last dynasty and of President Dawoud's.

The tragedy of Dawoud Khan's family reminded me of what my grandfather said to King Amanulla, 'The dynasty will end if the threat is from the inside.' That held true. The monarchy ended because of a takeover by a member of the royal family and that opened up the opportunity for other groups that sought power in Afghanistan.

My brother, living in Maimana with his ten kids, was very clever and escaped Afghanistan. He called me from Germany to sponsor him and bring him to the United States. Having his whole family in my house was not easy. I went to an army surplus store and bought ten cots for them to sleep on until they left. They didn't ask me for money to get out of the country. Fahima's family had lost everything they had after her father was put in jail, and had no money to leave the country. There were about six of them and they wrote asking for money for their travel expenses. It was tough because though the restaurant was doing enough business to stay open and pay our expenses; we did not have any extra cash or savings.

Herb Hafif, besides being our landlord, was a good friend. He always ate at *Walter's*, unless he was in court and one day at lunch he saw that Fahima and I were very disturbed. That was the day that I received the telegram from Fahima's parents requesting money. I didn't want to tell him, but he insisted. I finally told him the story. Fahima couldn't hold back her tears. Herb listened and tears came to his eyes and he left the room where we were sitting. The next day, Herb sent his secretary. She gave me an envelope and said, "Herb wants me to give this to you." When she left, I opened the envelope. There was a check made out to me with his signature but no amount. I didn't understand, so I went to his office which was nearby and asked him about it. He told me the check was for me and Fahima to get her family out of Afghanistan and we could write the amount for whatever the cost. I couldn't hold back my tears; neither could Herb. I will never forget that day.

We brought Fahima's family, and my brother and sisters to the United States. *Walter's* provided jobs and food for them all. Some still work for me and the rest after finding their way, went into other fields and businesses. They didn't go through what Fahima and I did when we came to California. We were established in Claremont and respected; people knew about our past and sympathized with their situation.

* * *

My father was an educated man; he believed in Islam; prayed, fasted and was honest. But never forced us to pray or fast. When I was a young boy he would talk about religion but always admitted that he did not understand the whole philosophy that some had that one religion was better than others. Maybe I adapted his philosophy, about religion, with a little variance. When I was a little boy and did something wrong, or didn't listen to my parents, at nights I thought I'd go to hell for those sins. I never heard that from my parents, but must have picked it up at school, on the streets or from servants. Then at the end of high school I became very doubtful of religion; almost an atheist. Not really knowing the whole theory or logic behind religion I was mostly confused and there was nobody who could explain things to me.

Just like in my political beliefs, I was not sure of my religious beliefs either. I didn't see things as black and white like a lot of people. I was always convinced that for this universe to be so orderly, for lack of any other convincing argument, there must be some kind of superior intelligence guiding and governing it all.

In my opinion, all religions taught the same thing except the name of their creator was different. People of different religions prayed differently and there are some other minor differences between them. But in my opinion, some clever people used those differences, focused on them and not the similarities, to make money and acquire status and position. The way I explained religion to my kids was through this analogy; there are many wonderful cuisines in the world. Each one is prepared and tastes differently but the ingredients come from the same vegetables, meats, starches, and dairy products (or combination) and the objective of eating them was to nourish our bodies, no matter what kind of cuisine we grew up with. Think of religion the same way.

It was not until late in my life that a friend of mine bought me a book which was a translation of Rumi's poetry from Persian to English. I heard of Rumi in high school and a part of his work was mentioned in Persian classes, but I never paid attention to the meaning of his poetry until I started reading the translations to English by Coleman Barks. The title of the book was *The Essential Rumi*. The beauty of Rumi's poetry, although not easy to understand, made me cry at times. I started reading and researching *Sufism*. In that I found what I was looking for.

What I perceived Rumi's thoughts to be was that God should be understood through love, not fear. You cannot understand God through reasoning alone, intuition is a part of it.

The god of all universes is the same God. All religions are different paths, arriving at the same destination. A true Muslim is not necessarily one who prays five times a day, does not drink, and so on. But is a person who connects to God directly, no matter what religion, or belief. A true Muslim or human being is not afraid of dying or fears the loss of material things. That is not the end of the world. In fact, a devout person believes that unless you disconnect with the material world, total tranquility is not possible.

Rumi states that the only way to overcome the fear of death is to die before you actually die. Of course I realize that I am a businessman living in America, where to most people acquiring wealth is the most important thing in the world. And the more wealth one has the more he or she wants. The more wealth one has, the more problems come with it, and I am probably in that same boat. But reading Rumi calms me down and gives me hope and I've found that music is also one way of worshipping.

I am not a religious person, but I am spiritual. I have been extremely lucky in life, and somehow the worst things that happened turned out to be the best things in my life.

When I was forced to go to military academy, I hated it but it turned out that I was the first one among my friends to come to America to study. I didn't return to my place of birth and disappointed my father; if I had returned. I would have been killed. The restaurant burned and I thought that our business career was finished, but it turned out that we rebuilt the restaurant better than it was before.

I honestly believe that my family and I have been protected by a power beyond my understanding.

* * *

My other business 'ventures'

I was always interested in bottling some of the chutney's and house dressings that we served at *Walter's* and also selling the homemade bread that we baked. Although we did sell them at the restaurant, my thought was that if I opened a gourmet shop, offered the bottled items, and added a few other specialty meats and pate's and cheeses, it could be a profitable business. I rented a place and improved it the way I wanted. It looked very good and for a few days we did have quite a few customers, but very soon the customer base declined. It was difficult to compete with the big supermarkets and discount stores and finally Fahima and I decided to close the shop and write off what we put into it.

As I mentioned previously, Fahima and Kay became very close. They went to cooking classes together, went out to restaurants often. Sometimes they invited me as well. Fahima and Kay had an idea in mind to open a pastry shop somewhere close to *Walter's* and provide gourmet desserts from their own recipes. At that time there was not one single decent pastry shop around Claremont. I took some classes for baking bread, and I wanted to add that to their store.

We opened the store and it went well for the first month. After that we couldn't break even and we closed the store and rented it out. I paid Kay her portion of the money back, and I took the whole loss. We learned a lot from that venture. Fahima and I couldn't be far from each other. Adding the pastry and bakery shop to the original *Walter's* was more profitable.

One good thing that came from this venture was we once catered a wedding and made good money from it. Fahima, Kay and I decided to spend that money just for us, since Herb couldn't join us because he was very busy. We decided to take a bike trip to the Loire valley in France. It was the first trip for me outside the US since leaving Afghanistan and I got introduced to fine dining and fine wines.

After that first trip we got hooked on biking as a group, not necessarily for sport, but an excuse to get away and have good food and wine. The most memorable trip was one to Vermont with only five of us: Fahima, Kay, Stan, Patty, and I. We biked at a time of the year when the leaves turned and the streets were full of color and stayed in an old bed and breakfast; beautiful homes and wonderful homemade food that I still remember.

One day on our trip we stopped to eat at a restaurant by a small river in Middleberry, Vermont. My friend Patty enthusiastically came to me, held my hand and said, "I'll show you something that you will like." I was wondering what it could be that made Patty so excited. She took me to this room where pictures of Afghanistan were on display by a local artist. As I was going through the pictures, I looked at them and all of a sudden memories of every place I had visited as a teenager came back. There were pictures of Paghman, Kandahar, Herat, and Maimana. The one from Maimana was of green hills during the spring time, exactly the way I remembered them. I fell in love with the pictures and asked a server who I could buy the pictures from. The girl came back and said that she called the artist who lived right around the corner, and he wanted to come and talk to me.

The artist, a young man with southern accent and long hair, arrived and greeted us. I introduced myself to him as an Afghan and told him that I wanted to buy all of his pictures. He was very nice and said, "I'm glad to sell them to you, but do you know how much they are?" I was so passionate about the pictures that I replied, "Does not matter, I will buy them." The artist saw my emotion and said that the pictures were done in an old Kodak method called dye transfer. Nobody does it like that anymore because it was a very time consuming method, but the color would not fade if taken care of. It takes a long time to develop one picture; therefore the price was very high. Only a few universities have them and they use it in classes. He invited me to his studio, and showed me the process. After that, he told me the price; he was right I couldn't afford them. I was disappointed and thanked him and left the studio.

To Lift a Mirror, for What You've Lost

He came to the restaurant after me and said since he felt I loved the pictures so much, he wanted to do something for me for free. He said that his brother was living in Apple Valley, California and he was planning to visit him. In a few months, he would ship all the pictures to me as a loan, and when he arrived, he would come and hang them in an order that explains Afghanistan's history, at no charge. Of course I accepted the offer. He showed up in a few months; the pictures were still in crates. He hanged them, and I invited a lot of people from the community to come and have dinner and enjoy the pictures of Afghanistan. The evening was very enjoyable for all my friends and neighbors. At the end, he came to me and said, "Keep the pictures for as long as you want. Enjoy them and return them to me anytime you feel that you no longer want to keep them." I kept them all for a few months, and wanted to return them, but couldn't. I called him and asked if I could buy the pictures and pay in payments. He agreed and I still have them in one of my restaurant's dining rooms. They have been in the same place since the Russian invasion of Afghanistan.

I asked him how he ended up in Afghanistan. He said it was a long story; he was working for his graduate degree in Archeology in Israel. The laws are so restrictive there that he couldn't accomplish much, so he took a month or so off, travelled to Iran and then to Afghanistan. He said he found Afghanistan fascinating; a bit of the modern world mixed with ancient. It was like he was back in the time of Jesus and Moses. He loved it, quit his work in Israel, went back to the US, took a course in photography and learned the dye transfer method. Then came back to Afghanistan and spent a year taking these pictures.

When he was in Claremont and busy with hanging the photographs till late at night, I invited him to stay with us rather than driving to Apple Valley, about an hour drive away. He accepted, so we went home and got ready to go to bed, but he kept talking. Fahima and I were very tired and had to get up early in the morning to work at the restaurant (although we don't cook or wait on tables anymore, we do manage daily operations). After a few yawns, he got the message and asked. "What kinds of Afghans are you, you work all day, go to bed early, and

123

you don't smoke hashish when you come home?" He was halfway right, we didn't smoke, but we did party until late on certain days of the week.

* * *

My second child

Fahima got pregnant with our second child when Asya was about seven years old. By this time we had to have someone from our family help Fahima. I was working all day and couldn't take time off from the restaurant. We wrote to Fahima's parents and told them about the news, and by the time she was eight months pregnant, her mother somehow bought a ticket and came to be with us during childbirth and for a few months afterwards to help out.

Our second child was a boy. Unlike Asya, who was very small, our boy was larger. This time I wouldn't make the mistake of not being with Fahima when she was delivering. I went so far as to be in the room while she was having the baby. I stayed for a while, but I saw some blood, or I thought I did, and heard her screaming. I quietly left the room and waited outside.

When he was born, I called *Walter's* to let the workers know that Fahima was fine and the baby healthy. All the customers cheered at the news since they knew us well. Some of those customers still come to *Walter's* and tell Dawoud, who is one of the managers; they remember the day he was born. He's 33 years old now.

When Dawoud was born, Fahima and I worked at Walter's seven days a week. Fahima worked until the day that I had to drive her to the hospital. Then I was left alone to cook, manage, clean and do whatever was needed in the restaurant, Fahima's mother who was came to help Fahima with the new born baby, volunteered to help me with cooking the few Afghan dishes we had in the menu, however she quit after she observed my style of cooking. I was mixing techniques of cooking from all over the world. Her style was very Afghan and her dishes were spicier and would take much longer to prepare.

To Lift a Mirror, for What You've Lost

Fahima was very happy, because of her mother helping her with the baby; the restaurant was left to me. Unlike Asya's care where I was the one who took care of her while an infant; I left Dawoud's care totally to his mother (and Asya).

Dawoud demonstrated a lot of potential in sports, even when he was in elementary school he was on top in tetherball. Later on when we became member of a club, he began to play and learn racquetball at the age of seven. When he was in his teens, he played all over the country in junior racquetball league and was ranked 5th in the nation.

Fahima and I picked the name Dawoud for him which is the biblical name David. For that reason if he chose to later on he could be called David by his friends. He did tell his friends in school that his name was David. Of course he looked different than the majority of his classmates in color and features, and they called him names. One day when he came home from school, he asked me, "Dad, Am I Jewish or something?" I asked him why he asked that question. He replied that his classmates call him that. Fahima and I, although we are Muslims, never pushed the religion on our kids.

Dawoud chose to go to public school and be with his friends unlike Asya who wanted to attend private school. Dawoud married a girl from a Palestinian-Jordanian background, so their wedding was very much done in the Afghan, Palestinian, American tradition.

Asya's wedding

My daughter Asya graduated from college and was still living at home. Unlike most other Afghan-American girls who were not allowed by their parents to have the freedom of going out (especially with boys who were not Afghan) we gave her a lot of freedom. We hardly told her what time to come home or restricted her in any way. However we did not think of her getting married anytime soon. I wanted her to finish graduate school first. But one day she surprised us by saying very casually that she loved this boy, who was not an Afghan, and she was going to marry him.

Fahima and I were shocked, but I was not Afghan enough to tell her that I forbid her to marry anyone without my permission, especially a non-Afghan. From the same belief, I was American enough to admit that she was an adult and should choose her partner as she wished.

Fahima and I accepted it. Asya arranged a meeting with Kurt. We took Kurt to a Chinese restaurant and after visiting and talking a little, to the surprise of Asya and Fahima, I told Kurt that if Asya chose him to be her future husband I would not stop her. But I would have been a lot happier if she chose an Afghan. (I regret what I said to this day, but they have forgiven me and I found Kurt to be the most wonderful husband, father and human being.)

Kurt is a true American with a Christian father, English and American Indian blood, and a Jewish mother. The whole family is extremely open-minded. Asya wanted to get married in both American and Afghan tradition, and Fahima and I were delighted to marry our only daughter in the old Afghan tradition. Although this was very different and unknown to Kurt's mother she accepted it.

The Afghan tradition is that the groom's mother calls on the parents of the bride to be and states the intentions of her son. The bride's parents then ask for some time to talk to their daughter and think about the proposal. In the mean time they are hospitable to the guests and offer them tea. However the tea is served without any sweets, which means that there is no agreement yet. In traditional Afghan household this practice continues for several days, the reason is to indicate that their daughter is not that desperate to get married. After this when they are ready to give their blessing and permission to their daughter; then they serve sweets with tea and that means they are ready to approve of the marriage. Of course we did not do that and served tea with sweets the first night.

In the old days, a boy and a girl married without seeing each other at all, and the marriages were truly arranged. So on their wedding night they went through a ceremony which is called *ayena mashaf*. In this ceremony the heads of both bride and groom are covered with a shawl and a mirror is put in front of them. They see each other for the first time in the mirror and it also means that the reflection of two becomes one. After that ceremony, the eldest of the family gets up and brings *henna* and puts it in the hands of bride and groom, and ties it with a previously prepared cloth. Afterwards the closest of family members and friends puts *henna* on their hands, as well. The Imam comes and marries the couple by asking the bride if she has agreed on her own free will to marry this man. He repeats this phrase three times and must hear a positive answer the third time. He then asks the parents of the bride if they have consented to this wedding. At the end of this ceremony the musicians sings traditional songs that are hundreds of years old to congratulate the wedding couple and entertain the guests.

Asya and Kurt both went through this traditional ceremony, but that was not enough, they had to get married the American way as well. That ceremony and wedding occurred on the lawn of the college where Asya and Kurt went to school and one of their professors married them.

* * *

My daughter married into an all-American family, where the girl's family pays for the wedding expenses, and my son married to a Palestinian family, where the groom's family pays for the wedding expenses. So being in America and having my kids marry the way they did, wasn't that good to me financially—something I still joke with them about today.

Asya's wedding

At Dawoud's wedding (Nangy, Fahima, Dawoud and Asya)

CHAPTER FOURTEEN
The Communist Takeover of Afghanistan

I was in graduate school when the news was announced that the Soviet Union had invaded Afghanistan. The presidential palace was taken and Dawoud Khan's family was murdered, including the children. Two of the children were hiding behind a curtain, when the soldiers who were searching the palace, noticed the curtain moving they fired into them with their machine guns killing the small children. Colonel Kader, who was in my squadron when I was in the Afghan Air Force, was present when the family was shot. Dawoud Khan didn't surrender and fired back at the people who wanted to capture him alive. The only survivor was his daughter-in-law, who was the sister of my first Afghan friend who came to Hollywood and rented an apartment from Fahima. She had been shot nine times and survived, but they murdered her children and husband. The whole family was buried in an unmarked mass grave on the outskirt of Kabul. The grave was found in 2009 and Dawoud Khan was reburied in a state funeral in March of 2009.

A meeting about the invasion was announced in graduate school and everyone attended. Professor Neal was the Soviet expert and gave a speech about the invasion. His conclusions were that Soviets had no intention of occupying Afghanistan. He said it was a defensive move, but that was not a satisfactory answer to me.

The whole Afghan community was all ears and eyes on the news every night, but unfortunately Afghanistan news, like any other news, loses momentum in our media. We all lost hope and thought that the Soviet empire gained another satellite country forced to submit to their ways. That was when I realized the true nature of the phrase, "dictatorship of the proletariat" (a phrase which the Russian communist party adapted to speed up the communist takeover of the world.) Thousands and thousands of people were killed, their houses burned, four million became immigrants, and one ethnic group was fighting another. The Soviet Union had controlled the central Asian countries for nearly 70 years; now one more state was added to that. Considering their military power, I didn't think that the Afghans would ever be able to push them out. It appeared that no other nations in the world cared either. Carter cancelled the Olympic Games, and that was it. Not much of a condemnation by the international community.

One day I was sitting in *Walter's*, drinking my favorite green tea when the brother of one of the merchants next to my restaurant came in for breakfast. After our introduction, (he knew from his brother that I was Afghan) I found out he worked for a government agency connected in some way to the Afghan Mujahidin. I asked him, "How are things going?" He answered, "If you asked me a year ago, I would have told you that there is no hope for the Afghans to get the Soviets out of their country, but now it is a different story. I think the Afghans have a chance." He was probably involved with arming or helping the Afghans or something that he didn't talk about, but he told me a story. He said he was teaching a class about battlefield tactics. A young man said, "That is very good, but how would I escape if that tactic does not work?" The teacher liked that answer and was convinced that Afghans were not just fighting to sacrifice themselves. The Mujahidin were getting stronger and ultimately made it so costly and untenable for the Soviets that they pulled out of Afghanistan after many losses.

The Mujahidin started planning their return to Afghanistan, and a friend of mine who was going to be in the cabinet of one of the interim presidents of Afghanistan called and invited me to go with them. I refused. Although I am proud of the bravery and sacrifice of the Afghan Mujahidin, they didn't do much good for the country. They fought among themselves, changed sides, killed innocent people, until finally the Taliban took control of most of the country in a short period of time. The United States almost recognized their regime. Then the first New York bombing occurred and President Clinton authorized cruise missile strikes that failed to kill Osama bin Laden. The Clinton administration asked the Taliban to give bin Laden to the west for trial. Of course they wouldn't give him up for the cultural reasons; *the pakhtoonwali code*. A Catholic priest who was helping in one of the

Afghan refugee camps told the west many times that the Afghans would not violate the code. Nobody listened.

The traditional *pakhtoonwali* code states that if someone asks for your protection, you shall never give him to the other side unless he voluntarily leaves your home. There is a story related to this.

A couple of young men quarreled in a bazaar and it got to a point where one used his gun and killed the other man. When the onlookers tried to capture and bring him to justice, he escaped and entered a residence and asked for refuge, which was given. The group of pursuers followed. When they found out that the man who was killed was the son of the house owner, they told him that the man he'd just given refuge to had killed his son. They asked the owner to let them take him so they could bring him to justice or that he himself should do the job. The house owner got angry and told the crowd, "What kind of Afghans are you? Don't you know the code? I cannot tell this man to leave my house nor can I punish him until he leaves, of his own free will." Even after the 9/11 horror, the reason Mullah Omar didn't hand bin Laden to the west was because of that code. They destroyed their own country, but the code was honored.

* * *

When the communist regime took over in Afghanistan, I helped many members of Fahima's family and my own get out of Afghanistan. The only ones left were my father and mother. Fahima and I decided to take a trip to India with the kids, and invite my mother and father to come to India, to see their grandkids and for my children to see their grandparents. I also planned to ask them to come to the United States and live with us for the rest of their lives. We arrived in New Delhi, and started calling. The telephone system in both India and Afghanistan was very bad, so I couldn't get in contact with them until the last day. I finally heard from them that the lines to the Indian embassy were so long that my mother and father didn't have the energy to wait in line for hours, so they gave up.

A year later, my mother called and said they were ready to meet me in India. I was very happy to go and get them. When I got there, I saw my mother but not my father. Although I was happy to see her, I thought that my father must have passed away and they never told me. When I asked where he was; my mother told me, "Your father has so much pride and is so patriotic that leaving his country in a time like this was unacceptable to him. Besides, he does not want his son and grandchildren see him so weak and incapable." I found out later that he had throat cancer and couldn't eat, and the doctors in Afghanistan were not capable of doing the operation he needed. If he had come with my mother I would have taken him to a doctor in India and he would have lived longer, but that was his choice. But my mother returned to the United States with us to stay with me for a while.

Before my mother came to live with us, Fahima's aunt came from Afghanistan and was already living with us. I had no choice but for them to become roommates in our guest house. Fahima's aunt being younger and there first, thought the guest house belonged more to her than my mother. My mother on the other hand, thought differently. She was always in command of the household back home and the house belonged to her son. She also felt my wife should not work and should dedicate her time to serve her just like in the Afghan tradition. Of course that wouldn't happen, and as much as I loved her she made things difficult for me.

Fahima's aunt didn't help much, with her selfishness and at times being mean to my mother. I asked my brothers to help but they didn't want any part of it. I finally rented a bungalow next to *Walter's* and hired a woman to stay with my mother and take her on walks in her wheelchair. Of course the restaurant was there, food was no problem, but I didn't have time to spend with her. When I put myself in her shoes, she had a miserable time. I have not forgiven myself for doing such a thing to my mother, but I had no choice. Keeping her in my house would have been difficult for my wife and I; she could manipulate me just as if I were a little kid. Finally my mother and the family decided that she should go back home, and of course I was there to take her back via Moscow, put her on Arianna Airlines and pay the steward a little money to take care of her.

About a year later my father passed away at age 81. Mother called again and wanted me to pick her up in Pakistan and bring her back to the United States. I went to Peshawar, Pakistan to pick her up where she was staying with my nieces and nephews who immigrated to Pakistan, because of the war. My daughter Asya volunteered to go with me and help bring her back to the United States.

All her life Asya had heard about Afghanistan; the simple life, the closeness of families, the friendships, and the simple beauty of the country. Stories from us that made her perceive Afghanistan as a great place. Asya had just graduated from college and was living in Santa Fe with her husband. Hearing that I was leaving for Pakistan, she called and wanted to go with me for two reasons: to help me and at the same time see if she could find a job to help the women in the refugee camps. We found a few organizations who were involved in helping Afghan refugees and there was a chance for her to get in touch with them in Peshawar. We visited the offices of these organizations to apply for a job for Asya. One man who was head of one of the organizations was very frank and told her that he wasn't sure what kind of job he could give her. She didn't speak Pashto (most of the refugees speak Pashto), she couldn't write or read either Pashto or Dari, and she had a very heavy foreign accent. Giving her a job in the camps as an Afghani was not possible, a job in an office as a secretary was not what she wanted, so that part of her trip did not work out.

We arrived and stayed in a continental hotel and Peshawar was amazing to Asya. We went to the bazaar almost every day and she found the people and customs fascinating. I rented a car and driver and went to the Department of Interior to get permission to go to the Khyber Pass and show Asya a little of Afghanistan, though we couldn't set foot there. The department gave us permission and a soldier to go with us, because it was in tribal areas. We drove through that fascinating pass, so full of history and legend, where most armies of invaders were defeated by the Afghans. And the armies of Afghans themselves used it as an invading route to India.

Asya and I travelled this route and I told her that her paternal grandmother came from one of these tribes. We arrived at Torkham check point on the border of Pakistan and Afghanistan. We both got out of the car and looked at the rugged, beautiful mountains on the other side of the border and I remembered the days when I and my friends came there during winter holidays and looked across from that side. We said that land belonged to Afghans and always would, no matter under which government. I couldn't stop my tears and felt so empty and helpless for not being able to go across to stand once again in my native country. At that time the communists were in power and if they caught me, I would be put in prison or shot. Asya cried with me and for me. We returned to our hotel in Peshawar and went to my nieces and nephews every night and visited my mother as we waited for the day of departure to come back home.

The people in Peshawar were extremely conservative; the women didn't go out after a certain time or not at all. I took Asya to a restaurant to eat and there was a section separate from the rest of the male customers for women to eat. Asya hated it. When Asya and I went back to the hotel we rented a three-wheel taxi. One night a policeman stopped the taxi and started asking questions and wanted to know about Asya's presence. I told him the truth that she was my daughter. He didn't believe me and thought she was a prostitute and spat on her face. When I showed him my American passport, he let us go. I used logic and didn't get emotional, but I was ready to kill him.

In the morning we told my family about it. They were so glad that nothing happened to us and suggested that we buy a calf, slaughter it, and give the meat to the poor. For God protected us from what could have been a very dangerous situation. The police of Peshawar were known to be corrupt and merciless. We did buy a calf and hired a butcher to come and do the job. Camera ready, Asya was very excited at first to see another thousand-year old custom of Afghans and Muslims; the sacrifice of a calf (originally it was a sheep, but any kosher animal is okay) for God. (This custom comes from a biblical story in the Bible and Quran where Ibrahim crucified his son Ismail when ordered to do it by God. Of course the story is a little different in each religion.) When the butcher started with the knife at the throat of the animal, Asya put the camera down and couldn't stop crying. I had to take her away from the scene.

Later when the butcher was finished with cleaning and cutting up the carcass, Asya came back so we could distribute the meat to the poor Afghan refugee families who were living in the compound. Asya started to take pictures of the women and when the Afghan women saw her, they all left in a hurry. Asya felt sad and thought that she must have done something to offend them or the Afghan culture. But in a few minutes the same women returned, their hair fixed and some with better clothes, and they let Asya take as many pictures as she wanted.

The day arrived when Asya, my mother and I would leave Peshawar for Karachi and from there to Los Angeles. We went to the airport, waited in line for four hours, and when it came time to go through passport control, one of the custom officers stopped my mother and told me that he wouldn't be able to let my mother go. She had a green card and everything was in order, but she didn't have a police permit to be in Pakistan. I laughed and said that there were more than three million Afghans in Pakistan and they all crossed the border. I didn't think any of them had a police permit. The customs officer told me, "Sir, nobody from Afghanistan is in Pakistan without a police permit." I told Asya to go ahead and get on the airplane. I would be home after I got things straightened out. She started crying and didn't move. I asked the customs officer to get his supervisor. The supervisor showed up, a tall handsome man in military uniform, with a curled mustache. He very politely asked me what the matter was. I explained to him the situation; he came close to my mother and talked to her courteously and asked a question or two, looked at her green card, and started speaking in Pashto. Seeing my name to be a pure Pashtun name, I was embarrassed to say that I was not very fluent in Pashto, but I was a Pashtun. He was a Pashtun as well. He gave a mean look to the customs officer and let both my mother and I join Asya on the other side. The custom officer's motive was to receive a bribe, which I was not going to give him.

CHAPTER FIFTEEN
9/11 and Afterwards

It was approximately 8.30 in the morning on the west coast when I received a telephone call that woke me. (Mornings from about 4.00 until 9.00AM are the best part of my sleep, because according to the doctors I have restless leg syndrome.) When I picked up the phone I thought that it had to be an emergency at *Walter's* for someone to call me when they knew that I would still be asleep. The caller, Patricia Kandell, a very close friend of ours from west L.A. (who was an early riser) asked me if I was watching TV. I told her, "No," I was still sleeping. She was almost in tears and told me New York had been bombed. It was like I was dreaming. Bombing New York? Who? Then she explained about the World Trade Center towers and the attack at the Pentagon and Flight 93 in Pennsylvania. It was a shock. My friends were worried about my family's safety because of our national origin, and of course being in business and known as Afghans.

I headed to *Walter's*. Fahima was at the club exercising. I got to the restaurant and saw the restaurant was empty, almost no customers. The workers were in shock too. We kept the restaurant open until nighttime, and I kept thinking that this would be the end of business for us. The Taliban in Afghanistan supporting al Qaida and the attacks were done by al Qaida who was in Afghanistan. And here we were Afghans and Muslims in America; even the owner of an Indian restaurant across from *Walter's* was scared. Someone killed a Sikh, because he had a turban, and was assumed to be a Muslim. My Sikh neighbor put note on his door: "I am not a Muslim, I am a Sikh."

A few days later, Fahima and I were at breakfast and very worried and depressed about what was going to happen. A group of people arrived at *Walter's* that we had known and served for years; the religious leaders of our town: a Catholic priest, a representative of the Mormon Church, other denominations of Christianity, plus the Jewish rabbi. They told us we shouldn't worry about anything and they would support us any way they could and assured us that we were an integral part of the community. I have tears in my eyes even now, as I write this many years later, because of that wonderful gesture by my neighbors. Although it is not perfect, I truly believe that there is no country like the United States of America where there is so much acceptance of differences in ethnicity and religion. Our friends advised us not to leave town, because if went someplace where others didn't know us, some crazy person could harm us. We treated the whole thing cautiously for a few months. We travelled to our vacation house in Laguna, where people would look strangely at us, wouldn't respond to our greetings and kind of ignored us, but our neighbors didn't show any reactions. The only place which I was discriminated against was at US Customs. When I was in India, I bought some musical instruments and shipped them home. I had to pick them up at a customs office in Long Beach. The process was bureaucratic. You had to go to an office, which brought the items to you, but before you picked it up, the custom officers had to inspect it. I went to one office, they sent me to another and back to the same office. They gave me dirty looks (I'm sure because it was right after 9/11 and I was an Afghan-American, a Muslim and was receiving a shipment from India) but finally agreed to look at the sent items. To really make me mad, they broke the bottom of the sitar in my shipment to look for bombs or drugs, which they didn't have to do.

* * *

The three things I enjoy in my life besides the love of my family and friends are music, sports, and travel. When it comes to music, I am totally Afghan. I do enjoy western music but I don't connect to it spiritually as much as I do to Afghan and Indian music. We were so deprived of it when Fahima and I first came to America. When we went for a drive in my old Chevrolet, especially in Alabama and Mississippi, I would sing for Fahima (though I am an absolutely horrible) all the songs that we both were familiar with. At that time when Fahima was homesick it sounded good to her and made me feel like I was not too bad of a singer.

To Lift a Mirror, for What You've Lost

When we came to California and began to know more Afghans, there were some who knew a little about music. We would get together on Saturday nights and they would sing for us. We danced and remembered old times. Our nights were long and the apartment managers were not very happy, but tolerated us. Sometimes we sat up all night and then went for breakfast at a Denny's or Norm's in Hollywood. We all did not have much, if anything. We lived in low priced apartments, had jobs that were beneath our abilities, but we had a good time. Later, especially after the communist occupation, more talented Afghan singers came to America, and we were financially in a position to have them in our houses for an entertaining night of music and food. We also had many concerts for our Afghan musicians at the restaurant as well.

The neighborhood I lived in later was a very exclusive neighborhood, with 100 years old homes built in a New England style. My neighbors were two professors from colleges that were very tolerant of our misbehavior. They tolerated our music for almost 20 years while we lived in that house, and when we moved still remained very good friends. They would come to the restaurant and one time they both told us that they missed us and our night music.

* * *

Walter's restaurant has been one of the ways we made friends with our neighbors and one of the instruments of our family's outreach to the community, as well. During the Soviet invasion and occupation of Afghanistan, Pomona Valley Hospital volunteered to do free surgery on some of the wounded Mojahids. They were brought to the hospital but the hospital food to them was very different. Congressman David Drier called me and asked me if I would donate food for the patients, and I gladly agreed. People who went to see these young Mojahids with me expected huge, rough people who fought against the Soviet army. When they saw these young, small people, they were amazed at their bravery. Unfortunately, today the same people are fighting against us.

The Afghan Soviet war made the Afghans very popular in America. People respected the Afghans and everybody thought that we were Mojahids. One time we went to a peace and freedom party function where a lot of rich people were members. The food was prepared by a famous chef, and they introduced Fahima and me as 'freedom fighters.' I looked at Fahima and she looked at me, and we both laughed. I started getting involved more and did a lot of charity parties at *Walter's* during its anniversary. Herbert Hafif did charity work at his house for many organizations and asked me to prepare the food. I accepted to do it at cost, and we included some charity organizations which were building schools for young Afghans. At times we were feeding 1500 people at one time. It was very rewarding; people liked the food and we collected a lot of money for Afghan children.

* * *

After 9/11 and the invasion of Afghanistan by American and NATO forces, Afghan interpreters were in high demand. I didn't like the idea of going with an army unit and seeing them shoot Afghans right in front of my eyes, right or wrong, so I was always against it and thought I would never do it. From the discussions at the Bonn conference the new government of Afghanistan went to Kabul. A friend of mine who I visited in Germany every year went to Kabul as an advisor on mining affairs to the Afghan president. When he got to Kabul, he told me to come and visit him. Fahima and I thought about it, and decided to go and visit Afghanistan for the first time in 40 years.

CHAPTER SIXTEEN
Back to Afghanistan (as a visitor)

In April of 2008, we decided to start the trip. First we went to Paris and spent 10 days, then through Dubai to Kabul. We arrived in Dubai around 11.00PM and the flight to Kabul was at 8.00AM the next morning. We had to report to Terminal 3, which was third class, three hours ahead of the flight. Fahima and I decided to remain in the airport and take a taxi from Terminal 2 to Terminal 3, that way we would be on time for our flight to Kabul. We got to Terminal 3 at about 5.00AM and already the terminal was full of Afghans dressed in local costumes and quite a few westerners as well. I already felt like I was home. People were not waiting in line; everybody was pushing the other to get ahead and looking to find somebody they knew with the airline authorities to get priority for boarding. I cannot put in words how nervous and excited we were to make this trip to the place of our birth.

At 8.00AM we boarded Safi Airlines for a two hour flight to Kabul. Although we had assigned seats, nobody followed the rules. A few westerners complained to the steward about their seat being taken. The steward, would say, "What's the difference? You will get to Kabul in two hours so there is no need to make the other guy get up."

I've already shared with you in the foreword my and Fahima's thoughts when we entered Afghanistan and landed at the airport outside Kabul. In Kabul there were more buildings of a Pakistani style of called Narco (they call them Narco architecture, because the money to build them comes from drugs and illegal sources), which was totally foreign to Afghanistan. Powerful warlords who acquired power and money during the civil war were stationed in Pakistan, came back home and since most were illiterate and had no knowledge about building, built any way they wanted.

The only things I recognized were the beautiful mountains around the Kabul valley. Once we left the city and crowds, the rest was not changed much. We took a trip to Shamali. It was incredible when we reached the Khyrkhana Pass. I remembered the days that we rode our bicycles to go to Kariz-e-Mir for swimming. The pass was now a city with thousands of homes, I am sure without a sewer system or running water, or any other services, but I could smell the clean air. It was winter and no dust. I didn't go to the king's farm, but I heard it had been destroyed.

A highway I once travelled to go to Bamyan with my friends had trees on both sides of the street for miles, but they were all cut down either by the Soviets (so the Mojahids could not hide under them) or natives as fuel to keep warm during the cold nights of winter. One incident which made me very upset was that this area was very famous for its vineyards. You could find a variety of grapes there and it was the greenest area of Kabul. When the Taliban came they burned all the vines so wine could not be made from them. My cousin told me that before the war an Italian company was making very good wines, and brandy from this area. Paghman was another disaster; most of the buildings were destroyed during the war and the whole area was taken over by a warlord. This man in the name of God and religion had taken everybody's property for himself. We drove to Qargha and found out that this area was also taken control of by another man and he had plans to make it a recreation center for himself on other people's property. The restaurant where I had dined before was closed.

We drove to Pangsher and found the highway in perfect shape. The Valley of Pangsher was breathtaking; the pass where the people of Pangsher stopped the Soviet army was full of destroyed Russian tanks. I found the people of Pangsher proud and independent. I got out of the car and had some spare money so I offered it to some kids who were around our car, but they refused to take the money. In Kabul if you showed money people would attack you.

The most enjoyable part of the trip to Pangsher was when we stopped at the base of Salang Pass. The road to the pass was built by the Soviets when I was still in Afghanistan but was closed during the war. My friend knew the owner of a restaurant at the base of this pass and called to tell him that we were coming. He slaughtered a sheep and kept the catch of the day from a river close by for us. When we got there we had the freshest trout and kabobs that I had had in a long time. We went to Jalalabad too. The road to Jalalabad was repaired by the Chinese and was a very nice road. It goes through a mountain pass which is beautiful; a river goes through where it falls hundreds of feet below. We reached Jalalabad and stayed in a government hotel that was built next to a palace of the late king. Next day we went to a Mojahid leader's house who was also a spiritual leader. We had lunch with him, and then drove to Torkham, the border town which divides the Afghan tribal people. This was the same area where I brought Asya from Peshawar.

The sad part was to see the immigrants, those who fled the war, return to Afghanistan. After the Taliban and Soviets left the country, they came back to their home, but when they saw them destroyed, no jobs and a weak dysfunctional government, they returned to the refugee camps in Pakistan.

* * *

The Serena Hotel is the only 5-star hotel in Kabul. I believe it was built by Agha Khan, who has a lot of followers in Afghanistan, especially among Hazaras. The hotel was built in the same location where the Kabul Hotel was. When you arrive your car is checked for bombs and you go through electronic screening. Once inside, you feel like you are not in Afghanistan although the decor is done in a beautiful Afghan style with handicraft pieces of carved wood and carpets from all regions of Afghanistan. The dining room serves western style food, served by an Asian staff, and I believe the management is also from abroad. What I heard was that after seven years of operation, the hotel would be handed to the Afghan government, so Agha Khan was making the best out of it. The room prices are as high as $500 to $600 dollars a night and the food buffet is around $30 dollars a person. You see people with their laptops everywhere. Deals are made in this hotel; the important people of Kabul are seen here.

My cousin and her husband are very close to the late monarch's family in Kabul. The king was still alive, but not in a good health. We met the princess and her daughter in a private area of the hotel and my cousin invited them for afternoon tea. When we went the next day, in return she invited us for afternoon tea. I also met the crown prince one night; a very nice man, we spent a lot of time that night talking about how much he missed his family who were still in the United States.

Leaving after two weeks in Afghanistan made me think about how I could help my country of birth in some capacity. Something where I wouldn't be a part of the Afghan administration yet still be able to make a difference, but I couldn't think of anything.

Fahima on the other hand was very disappointed with the situation; seeing beautiful kids beg on streets, the women totally covered and without rights... for her this was the last trip. She stated that emotionally she would not be able to take another trip back. For her there was not a choice; however she would do things in the United States to promote the cause of the Afghan people.

CHAPTER SEVENTEEN
Returning to Afghanistan (as an advisor)

2008 was a terrible year for many in the restaurant business. The fall of real estate values, the deepening recession, affected all. People just were not eating out as often and sales were down at *Walter's*.

One day a friend of mine mentioned that he worked with a company recruiting qualified people to go to Afghanistan as an advisor for the Department of Defense (DOD). He told me there were no obligations, just sign up and you can cancel any time. What he shared with me was in the back of my mind for a couple of months and finally I mentioned it to Fahima to get her reaction. Everybody in my family was against me doing this, but deep down I wanted this opportunity to go back to the country of my birth, not as a tourist, but to do something positive. Working with the government of Afghanistan was out of the question as was being part of the war effort. But to go as an advisor, to help communicate and bring peace to Afghan communities was very much something I wanted to be part of. I kept pushing the idea to my family and the decline in business helped a lot. I finally convinced my family and half-heartedly they said I could go.

I called my friend and told him I was interested and wanted to apply with the company he was representing. It took about two months to hear back. He called to tell me the company he was working for didn't get the DOD contract, but another company did and his partner was now working with the other company. He would see that my application was reviewed by them. A month later I got a call from a woman with the company, asking me questions about my background. She wanted to know if I was still interested in the job. After listening to her, I was suspicious of how she got my name and my information. I told her to call me back in a few days and I would have an answer for her. I called my friend and wanted to know what the deal was. He told me that his partner had stolen the file with the applicants resume's from the company that did not get the DOD contract and given them to this other company he was now working for. My friend told me, if I still wanted the job, it was okay with him to go ahead. The women called me back and asked if I had made my decision. I said I would accept the job and wanted to know about the interview. She said that her phone conversation with me was all that was necessary. I didn't need an interview and I would get a job offer by the next day, which I did. I accepted the offer and now had to fill out forms and paperwork they had sent me for a security clearance. After that, I was given a date to report to Fort Benning in Columbus, Georgia for preparation to be shipped out to Kabul.

Before going to Fort Benning, I got a call from the company's head of recruiting who told me that the position I had been assigned was a very important one. I would be stationed in Kabul in a camp where I would be advising General Officers on Afghan culture. The camp had a bar, a racquetball court and private rooms and I would have my own driver. This was something that I didn't expect, but it made me happy. So I packed my racquetball racket with some gloves and balls, thinking that I would have time to play.

***

The day arrived when Fahima took me to the airport for my flight to Columbus, Georgia. I met my friend Baray in the hotel in Columbus, who would be with me in the same program for one year. It was great news for both of us. We lived in southern California, had partied together and had mutual friends, but above all we both had the same point of view about Afghanistan. We spent a week going through orientation at the hotel, then to Fort Benning for our medical exam. The medical exam was very thorough and when they X-rayed my lungs, they saw a little scar on one. That could have been a cause to deny me clearance to go to Afghanistan, but this scar had been in my lung for more than 60 years. I must have had pneumonia at a young age. It was discovered when I first came to the United States when I was 19. The Afghan doctor thought nothing of it, but I had to prove to the military doctors it wasn't a health issue. I phoned my family doctor to send my records and once they reviewed them I was cleared. Another thing happened that could have stopped me from going to Afghanistan. Fort Benning had racquet ball courts and one night after the physical exams I decided to go and play. I played two young soldiers and hit the front wall with my foot, breaking my large toe. If I reported that I'd hurt myself I would have been disqualified, so I hid it with the help of my friends.

At Benning we were issued sleeping bags, armored vests and other essentials. Next we were sent to a Florida facility to qualify in handling small arms. We stayed there for three days. In the mornings we learned about weapons and safety and in the afternoon we were on the range firing our weapons. At the facility there was one room where we all watched TV. One day my friend turned the station to CNN to listen to the news. Almost all the other people in the room yelled at us to change the channel because they didn't want to listen to a communist channel. My friend and I realized we better do what these former military men said or we might get killed before we get to Afghanistan. The people going to Afghanistan consisted of two groups, Afghan–Americans as cultural advisors, and ex-armed forces as military advisors.

I can't remember when I first used a gun; I believe it was in the Afghan military academy almost 50 years ago. At the range, the first day I was next to another Afghan who had been to Afghanistan before and knew his way around. The targets were assigned to each of us and we got in position and started shooting. When we had fired all the ammo we'd been given, the firing stopped and you and the range officer were allowed to inspect the target to see if you qualified. The guy next to me and I went to see our results. He had almost 70 hits on his target, and I had none. I got very discouraged; I used to be a military man and this was ridiculous. We both fired 40 rounds each and I should have gotten at least some rounds on the target. What we found out was that I fired at his target. That made me feel a little better but the officer, instead of dividing the rounds between us disqualified us both. We had to do it all over again and the guy who'd been next to me was not happy.

Weapon qualification camp in Florida

The day arrived when we had to depart for Kabul with a stop in Dubai. We spent the night at Dubai airport and at 8.00AM took a flight by Safi Airlines to Kabul, which got us there early in the morning. Kabul Airport looked a little different from my trip two years before, but the broken aircraft around the airport, the atmosphere of uncertainty and hungry porters fighting to get our luggage made me sad for my country and the Afghan people all over again. A couple of people from our team who arrived in Kabul a few weeks earlier met us at the airport to take us to Green Village. They were extremely nervous driving through the streets. There were suicide bombers in Kabul recently, so they were right to be nervous.

We arrived at Green Village and it was nothing like I thought it would be. I assumed our "camp" would be military, but it turned out to be a complex owned by a Russian with an Afghan partner, who hired Korga people from Nepal as security guards. The head chef was from one of the Balkan countries and the kitchen workers were local Afghans. The camp was full of other nationalities. Recently there had been an attack on a U.N. compound in Kabul, so all the U.N. personnel were moved to Green Village. The construction in the compound was ongoing just to meet the demand for housing. The rooms were adequate, and the compound did have a bar, a racquetball court and massage parlor with masseuse from central Asian countries.

We stayed in Green Village for a week for orientation and assignments. The management of this company was just as new as we were, so we all learned through trial and error. We were warned not to go to town and Baray and I had many contacts in Kabul we were not allowed to see. We were disappointed and I felt after spending many years of my life in management and accomplishing so much, to be ordered around by someone who was not qualified, that I was more of a prisoner than an advisor.

One day a manager came to Baray and me and said that a vacancy just opened up in northern Afghanistan and he wanted us to think about it. Baray and I looked at each other and in a matter of a few minutes decided that it couldn't be worse than Green Village. We accepted the offer and a few days later flew to Mazar-e-Sharif for our assignment. Baray and I were assigned to the headquarters in Camp Marmal located on the outskirts of the city.

Mazar-e-Sharif was the H.Q. for all of the PRTs (provisional reconstructions teams) in the north of Afghanistan, which includes, Badakhsan, Fiazabad, Kunduz, Baghlan, Balkh, Jozjan and Faryab. The H.Q. was run and operated by Germans and like a complete city, had its own airport, sewer system and even deep wells to bottle its own water. In the camp the soldiers were Norwegians, Croatians, Swedes and Macedonians, just to name a few of the nationalities.

Afghan assignment

The last time I was in Mazar-e-Sharif was in the 1950s with either my brother or my mother. We travelled to the city from Kabul in a truck and spent the night or nights with relatives from my mother's side. My uncle used to live there until he died and his children lived with their mother until she died. Then my cousins and nieces lived with their maternal uncle for a short period of time until my mother found out that one of my nieces at age nine or ten was sold by her uncle to a grown man to be his wife. That's when she rushed to Mazar, took the kids and brought them to Kabul. My father and mother adopted all four and they lived with us. One of my favorite nieces who now lives in the United States became my roommate. She was a bright girl, helped me with my homework and became like an older sister.

Mazar had changed tremendously and had become a big city compared to how I knew it from years ago. There were many high rise buildings of all sorts being built all around the city; more Narco architecture because the buildings are owned by warlords or drug dealers. The governor of the province was a very strong man who kept the city safe from Taliban attack but recently the city was becoming more dangerous to live in. The coalition forces liked him and he cooperated with the central government. The word on the streets was that he had ties with the insurgents as well as drug dealers. He was the richest man in the province and had a lot of support among the Tajeks. After the 9/11 invasion, he helped in the operations against the Taliban. The city was booming with multi-floor office buildings and very expensive houses. We were invited to a very rich man's house and there he talked about the millions of dollars he had and wanted Baray and I to become his partners to help him get contracts for him from the coalition forces, and then he would do the rest.

On the other side of town things weren't as good for the people.

One day in that part of the city I was sitting on a bench and a little boy who couldn't have been more than nine or ten years old approached me for a shoe shine. The price was 10 Afg. I agreed and asked the kid about his family and why he was not going to school. He responded that his mother needed help to pay the rent and he did not have a father. He spent all day on the streets to make the equivalent of two dollars.

On one of the trips to find out about life in Mazar-e-Sharif, we (an Afghan-American lady and I) made an appointment to go to a local women's prison run by the Afghan police, who were all male. The prison was the size of two small bed rooms; in its small yard was a tent. The prison held about 40 women plus their children. A few of the kids were school age and had been in the prison with their mothers for two to three years. They were prisoners as well. We also observed that a few of the women inmates were pregnant; even though these women had not been out of the prison for at least two years.

We went back to our camp and convinced the American Army to give us some money to spend on the prison. The Lieutenant Colonel, a wonderful young officer, provided funds and the next day, the lady and I went shopping. We bought sewing machines, tables, chairs, material, books, notebooks, pen and pencils, toiletries and many other things. We wanted to provide the women a way to keep busy and also a means to learn a living such as sewing.

Returning to the prison, by the time we unloaded the merchandise, half of it was stolen by the prison commander and his staff right in front of our eyes. We couldn't stop them; our only option was to write a report to their superior and let them know what happened. The report was written and given to them, but we never heard what was done about it if anything.

One of the biggest surprises was the availability of modern products in the city: computers, televisions, air conditioning units, construction machinery, and medicine of all sorts. You name it and it was there in the bazaars. All you needed was money, which only the rich had. Unfortunately the local maternity hospital lacked a lot of things like gowns for the patients, medicine for the women and children, benches for the patients to set and wait, and blankets for the new born, just to name a few. We provided those items with the help of the American Army.

* * *

In one of my side-trips in the Faryab province, during the spring time when the rivers were flooding, I went to a village with one of the American patrol teams. The Humvee I was in got stuck in the river during a night crossing. We usually moved at night to change positions and in a blackout condition which means that all lights, including vehicle, are off so the insurgents couldn't see us. Only the driver had night vision goggles on to see and when wearing them you have virtually no depth perception. So we entered the river from a steep angle, got stuck and the water came to our waist. When we finally made it out of the river, with another Humvee pulling us, I got out of the car and dropped and lost my glasses in the river. The only other pair I had was my prescription sunglasses, which I couldn't wear at night and I was stuck with the group for several days.

When I got back to Mazar, one of my friends told me that he saw a store sign in the city which had a picture of glasses. I went there the next day and inquired about glasses. The owner said no problem he could make a pair for me. He asked me if I had the prescription, which I didn't. I asked where I could get my eyes examined. Again, he said, "No problem." He took a tray of lenses out of his drawer and put a few on my eye, then told me to read the sign on the side of a truck parked outside of the store. One of the lenses finally was clear enough for me to read the sign and a day later he gave me the pair of glasses. The whole thing with the frame cost me $25.00 USD and I was more than satisfied.

* * *

Soon after arriving in the city a friend and I wanted to eat in a local restaurant. We ended up in a restaurant where everybody would sit on a platform, take their shoes off and eat with their hands. Although we both grew up in Afghanistan, we had never dined like this but enjoyed it. The kabob and rice pilaf was excellent, and the northern Naan or flat bread was different than the Kabuli style, but just as delicious.

Nangy (on the left) and Baray Karim in a local restaurant in Mazar-e-Sharif

At a restaurant in Pol-e-Khomri

There were other restaurants for foreigners to go to, but they were more expensive. These restaurants were secured with barbed wire and security guards and mostly served either western food or Indian food and served alcohol but only to foreigners. One Afghan had opened up a restaurant and tried to westernize the menu but it was terrible food. It wasn't Afghan or western, but the restaurant itself had a very good ambience and was decorated with Afghan art and crafts.

* * *

In the city, the Shrine of Hazrat Ali (which coalition forces refer to as the blue mosque) had not changed, it was still beautiful. A religious and historical monument in the center of the city it was built in the 12th century, destroyed during the Mongol invasion, then rebuilt in the 15th century. Legend has it that Hazrat Ali, the fourth Caliph of Islam, cousin and son-in-law of prophet Mohammad, was said to be buried in the city of Kofa (in today's Syria). The ruler of the Balkh province in the 12th century one night dreamed that Hazrat Ali told him his body was buried in the ruins of Balkh, and ordered him make a shrine for him in the city. The king told the Imam of his mosque about the dream and asked for an interpretation. The Imam replied it was a satanic dream and should be ignored because history was clear that Ali was buried in Kofa. The ruler was convinced and did not heed the message until he dreamed again. This time Hazrat Ali grew angry and told him the exact location of where the body could be found. The ruler sent his soldiers to dig at the location. They found the body and the ruler built the mausoleum and shrine. Some say that a famous mason was brought from India to do the work.

To Lift a Mirror, for What You've Lost

Mausoleum of Hazrat-e-Ali in Mazar-e-Sharif

* * *

The company I worked for wanted to send a team to Maimana. It was in work for a couple of months until the agreements were in place with the Norwegian command. Maimana, which was also the name of the province in old times, now is the capital of Faryab province. The coalition country responsible for that province is Norway. They had established a PRT (provisional reconstruction team) on the outskirt of the city. They asked me if I wanted to go there, but saw that my position was too high for that slot, so the compromise was that I divided the whole northern section of Afghanistan into two parts and gave one to my friend Baray, who was the next highest level. I kept the portion which had Maimana and then I could travel there, assist and then come back to my Mazar position where I was stationed.

Although we changed a lot of procedures and rules while working in Mazar-e-Sharif, the structure of the company was that there was an office director, an editor, a senior cultural advisor, a senior special advisor, an Afghan advisor and a military advisor in our team. The way it was set up was that the office director and the military advisors were ex-military personnel who either served in Iraq or had some military background. They could have been great soldiers in their time, but as far as management, culture and human relations, they had only fundamental knowledge and little experience. While the cultural and special advisors had masters degrees or beyond, and knew all or a few of the Afghan languages. We were managed by these inexperienced young men, who absolutely had no idea about the culture or how to approach the Afghan public.

Perhaps it is not fair to generalize, but the people who managed and directed the teams broke all the laws of the country, especially when they were driving. They would cut off everybody, drove 100 KMPH on a street where 20 KMPH was too fast and wouldn't stop for law enforcement. Yet were there to teach Afghans to obey the law, and respect other people's rights. On occasions these managers treated like 2nd class citizens the Afghan-Americans who were the only tools for making this program successful. Many intelligent Afghan-Americans quit the company and joined other companies who were more sensitive about these matters.

* * *

A vacation break

In April of 2010, I had been in Afghanistan for more than six months and was eligible for a ten day vacation. The vacation time was so short that I called Fahima and we decided to meet in Rome, our favorite city, then rent a car and go to Positano Beach, just her and me. That way I didn't have to meet a lot of friends and family back home and not have enough time with her. I flew to Rome and went to the hotel and was very anxious to meet Fahima the next day at the airport. The next morning I took the train to the airport and waited but the flight didn't show up.

Because of the volcanic ash out of Iceland, hundreds of flights were cancelled, and Fahima's was one of them. I stayed alone in Rome for seven days and Fahima stayed with her aunt in London. Thank God for her aunt, otherwise she would have had a horrible time. Fahima ended up crossing the channel on the "chunnel" train and a friend got her an expensive flight from Paris to Rome. She told me that going from the train station to the airport was another adventure. She had so little time that if she hired a taxi, she would have never made it to the airport on time. So she hired a guy who put her and her luggage on the back of his motorcycle and got her to the airport in time to make her flight to Rome. At least we were able to spend a couple of days together. While she was still in London I became such an expert on sightseeing in Rome I could take a job as a guide. I walked to every historical sight possible in Rome throughout the time that I was there.

After our couple of days together, it was time for Fahima to go back to California and I took her to the airport. She departed without any incident. My flight was later that afternoon, to Vienna to take a connecting flight to Dubai. The flight to Vienna was not a long one. We took off and after about 15 minutes in the air I heard a squeaking noise in the body of the airplane. Nobody else paid any attention but me. Soon afterwards, the announcement came that the airplane was going to return to Rome due to mechanical problems. Although not very serious the nose landing gear didn't retract properly and the landing gear cowling was making the noise. We returned to Rome and had to be assigned a different flight to Dubai. The flight I was assigned to was very luxurious and debarked at a very modern, clean, and lavish terminal that I had never used before in Dubai where I changed terminals to board Safi Airlines for my flight to Kabul.

* * *

I landed at Camp Marmal, which was the headquarters of the German forces in Afghanistan. We were picked up by a couple of people from our team and then driven to the barracks. I roomed with an Air Force major who was from San Jose, California. We had good chemistry from the beginning. He helped me make my bed and the first night we stayed up till 2.00AM in the morning and got to know each other. We agreed on a lot of issues about world politics and so on. I had another flash back from my days going through different schools in the air force and sharing a room with other people. To be honest, I felt younger and at home.

Back home in the US the life style was different. We were always focused on buying bigger homes, remodeling bathrooms, kitchens and living rooms. Now I was living in a room approximately 20x10 feet with two people and all their belongings and I felt satisfied. We cleaned it ourselves every morning. My roommate had a water boiler so we made tea and occasionally bought a bottle of wine from the German commissary to drink secretly because we were not allowed to drink.

The German camp is probably an area of five miles square in the middle of a desert, but the Germans were extremely organized. The camp had a church, mosque, commissary, airstrip, a couple of restaurants, and a beer and wine bar. On the other side of the camp was the Norwegians. They had their own mess hall and pizzeria and commissary, and we could eat in either one. There were soldiers from

Sweden, Hungary, Croatia, Macedonia, Italy, and France just to name a few; however the commander of the post was a German General. The deputy commander was an American and the chief of staff was a Norwegian.

Recently with the Obama surge, Camp Marmal has expanded in size almost twice as large in order to make room for the American forces, so there was one more mess hall, an American dining room. I was very surprised to see some great Southern style catfish in the buffet line (I love catfish). The way I prepare it at *Walter's* is a copy of Wolfgang Puck's recipe; marinated in soy sauce with slices of fresh ginger and fresh garlic alternated in the body of the fish, coated with corn starch, then fried. There was also an Afghan restaurant by the gate where most of the day workers ate. We ventured there a few times and it was very unsanitary, but had tasty food. They had three kinds of kabobs and pilaf with carrots and raisins. They prepared it a little different than I do, but it was still very good.

The morning after we arrived Baray and I were introduced to the other staff of the office. We had a good reception and they were very happy to have Afghan-Americans, who knew the culture, with them so they could connect with the locals. Up to then people from our outfit had no contact with the locals. They were in Afghanistan, but were kind of imprisoned inside the camp. I saw this as a failure of our efforts to win the hearts and minds of people of Afghanistan. You have to know them and their culture and also for them to know about us and our culture. Most of the people in our chain of command didn't know this and we got into arguments. My friend Baray and I almost resigned from our positions. People who were in charge of our program were young and extremely tunnel-visioned when it came to public relations regarding Afghan culture and diplomacy and so on. Most were ex-military. They would have been great in that field, but were almost useless in what they were currently tasked to do.

The US Army officer who was in charge of the program was a very brilliant man and our supporter. He encouraged us to build relations with the local elite. So for the first time we were allowed to go to the city and engage with people and our idea was to invite local people to the camp and socialize with them and show them our way of life. I volunteered to cook the first American dinner for our Afghan guests. We invited several college professors, businessmen, and others from MeS (Mazar-e-Sharif) to have dinner with us. The menu was steaks, baked potatoes, veggies; the salad was a lettuce, Feta cheese, pine nuts, fresh corn, assortment of blackened bell peppers, and bruschetta's. Nachos for appetizers and apple pie and ice cream for dessert. Of course I was the cook, with a couple of soldiers with two left hands for assistants.

The dinner from my point of view was awful. The steak was dry, the vegetables were soggy, and the potatoes cold and moist. That night it rained heavily. I had barbequed steaks in mind but ended up cooking the steak in the German kitchen in an oven. The appetizers were good, and the pie was brought frozen from home for military personnel and it was alright. Guests raved about the food. Maybe they just wanted to be nice. After that party the camp adapted the program and wanted us to do more in order to establish cultural ties with the Afghan community.

We were only in Camp Marmal for two weeks when one night I woke up with extreme pain in my lower back on the right side. I diagnosed it as kidney stones, because a few years back it had happened to me and I had called 911 to take me to the hospital. So I recognized it. I didn't know where the hospital was and I didn't have a car even if I did. I woke up my neighbor because my roommate was on a mission. My neighbor took me to the emergency room. The young lady soldier after hearing my story told me there was nothing she could do because the doctors did not come to work until 8:00AM. So I should return to my room and come back later. I couldn't believe this was a German field hospital, equipped with modern medical equipment and specialists, but I had to go back to my room and suffer for another six or seven hours. I came back at 8:00AM and the Urologist immediately examined me. I told him what time the pain started and he was furious that the nurse didn't call him. He apologized for that and later I found out that the nurse just arrived a few days ago and didn't know the

160

correct procedures. I was hospitalized and he inserted a catheter and left it there for 10 days. While I was in the hospital the hospital chief and his staff, plus the nurse who sent me home, came to my bedside and asked for my forgiveness for having suffered so much the night before.

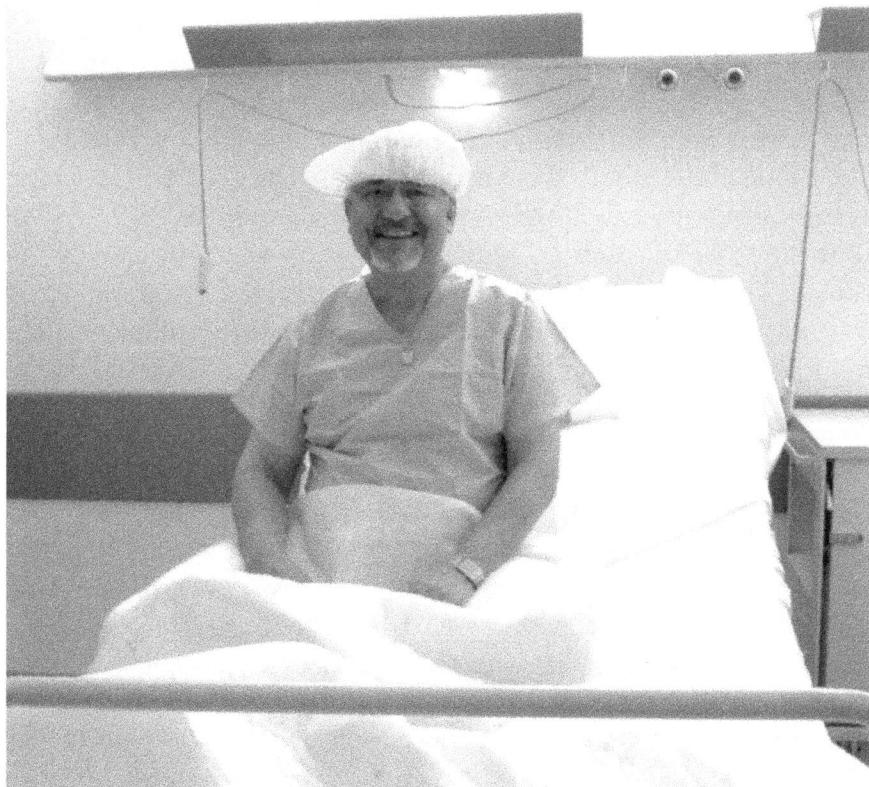

At the German field hospital in Camp Marmal Mazar-e-Sharif

CHAPTER EIGHTEEN
Maimana

Maimana is one of the places that I treasure. I spent my childhood and teenage years there. I took a 45-minute German flight to Maimana early in the morning. The weather was crisp and clear and as we got closer to the city, I saw the rolling hills of Jozjan, Andkhoy and Maimana. It brought unforgettable memories of my teenage years back to me. The airport was located in the northern part of the city and the airplane landed on a dirt runway that didn't exist when I was there in my childhood. The PRT (provisional reconstruction team) camp commanded by Norwegian forces was very small and used to be in the city. But after a caricature of Mohammad showed up in one of the Scandinavian newspapers, thousands of demonstrators showed up at the gates of the PRT. After the demonstration, the Norwegians decided to move to a more secure camp next to the airport.

As I found out the first day that I left the camp to go to town, it was located only about 7 kilometers from my family's land. I recognized it after I saw the river next to the camp and thought, 'my God, this river was the one that I crossed with my horse late at night when I returned to the family ranch from the city.' Now the river was different. A Korean company had dredged it in search of gravel and had made gigantic holes everywhere, leaving the river looking like it had been bombed. At one point they had dug so deep that it was very dangerous to cross but they built a crossing there anyway. We all knew it was going to collapse and when the flood came that crossing fell and the locals and military vehicles had to detour through the narrow village roads, scraping the walls of the locals, which made them very mad.

I ventured to town a few times and found it very different as well. The places I went with my friends, to sit in the café and play *carromboard*, (a finger pool game played on a 29 inch by 29 inch board with four pockets) and see an Indian movie (the only kind they showed), were destroyed by the Taliban for being un-Islamic. The streets were paved now, but didn't have the feeling of what I remembered. It used to be a clean, primitive, unique, innocent town with horses and donkeys. It had public baths where I used to go and it was so hot inside that we ordered watermelon which was very cold in the winter. Now that was all gone. The donkeys were still there, but the horses were replaced by filthy put-puts and motorcycles and a lot of cars. One day I rented a taxi with a steering wheel on the right side and asked the driver how he could drive when it was illegal. He laughed and said, "It is very simple. When I get stopped by a traffic cop I pay him—he lets me go—I continue my business until I get caught again."

My biggest desire was to visit Kariz Qala (in Persian *qala* means a fort or castle), our family land that my brother now owns. He was not there in Maimana, but I couldn't wait and told him to call his foreman and let him know I was coming with a bunch of friends to visit. I had helped my brother come to America with his ten children. They lived in Los Angeles for a few years and when his daughter got married to a man who lived in Las Vegas, he packed his bags and left for Vegas with his family. He was an engineer, but the only job he could find in Vegas was driving a taxi. He got very frustrated and without consulting anyone decided to return to Afghanistan and claim our land from the Taliban. First he grew a beard and then came to Maimana where he convinced the governor of the Taliban that his land was taken from him by the communists. The governor ordered all the people who were on the land to leave. We were all shocked and speechless when we heard the news. He came back to the United States for his wife and returned with her to live on his land.

I couldn't wait to get to Kariz Qala. Instead of being on horse as I was last time I visited, this time I was in a Humvee. When we crossed the three rivers I remembered every inch of the road where I used to cross with my horse. There were a few modern looking buildings which were built by the coalition forces, but the rest of the land and mud houses were the same. When I got to the village I couldn't stop talking to the Norwegian soldiers who were with me about the small forest on the land and the Qala that my grandfather built.

Again disappointment at the changes was what I felt instead of seeing what I remembered. My brother built a new two-storey house where the forest area used to be. Its trees were so thick when I was there last that we couldn't venture inside the forest for fear of wild boar, coyotes and other wild animals. I remember when it was snowing I would take my brothers shotgun and go in the woods and blindly shoot into the trees and get many birds. The small black birds have very sweet meat and I would bring them home and cook them on an open fire. I didn't see much wildlife this time anywhere and now not one tree existed. The new house, while not bad if it was in Mexico or Pakistan, was out of place. Next I wanted to see the Qala. It was the saddest part of my visit. The beautiful wooden door was broken into pieces. Inside the tall walls no building remained. They were all destroyed. The family compound, the stables, the servant's house, was all a mound of dirt. During the wars each side would take control of the Qala and make it their headquarters. When they fought the first thing that got destroyed was the Qala. Eventually everything was so devastated that nobody wanted to repair it.

In the village I met a man who as a boy I remembered playing with when I was very young. I remember those days so clearly that it seems impossible that so much time has passed. He looked very good. He had some problem hearing when he was young that still existed but hadn't deteriorated. He took me to see his mother who was still alive and active at age 92. She lived with her daughter who looked old and was not as lively. They embraced me and were very happy to see me. This sister was older than the rest of us and I recalled for them that when we would come back from playing she would strip our clothing off and wash all the mud from our bodies and clothes before letting us inside the house. She told me a story that I had forgotten. There was a domesticated deer or elk that would come inside the yard every night. My young brother, Barry, who rode small ponies without a saddle, would climb on the back of the elk inside the yard. One day when the gate was open he was riding the elk and it was time for it to go to the forest to gather food. The elk took my young brother, who wouldn't get off him, to the forest. My mother and the servants panicked and all ran after them, but when the servants got close to the dense area of the forest they found Barry on the ground crying but unhurt. He had fallen off.

The land itself with the rolling hills inside the perimeter was still as beautiful as I remembered, even the places where I rolled all the way down with my friends. I remembered one time I was coming from the city to Kariz Qala, not by the rivers but by another trail through the foothills. The trail was almost empty and at one bend I saw a fox way up on the hill. When I turned the corner on my horse there was the fox right next to me and keeping the same pace. Just to see what the fox would do I stopped the horse. And the fox would stop. When I started going the fox started walking. I got off the horse and the fox ran to the hill and disappeared. When I got back on the horse the fox was right next to me. It was just playing with me until I got close to a village, then it disappeared.

The village people came to see me, but I didn't recognize anyone. When I asked them if they were so and so they answered that I had mistaken them for their father and he had passed away. They looked so old. Years of war and misery had aged them terribly beyond their years. The foreman prepared a lot of food for us. We ate quickly because we had to leave before dark. The most important thing that had been lost was the peaceful nature of this area. After dark the insurgents controlled it and we would not be safe. It made me wonder if God must be very mad at Afghans to let this happen.

The war had changed people's opinion toward each other. A policeman from the city of Maimana used to be able to safely walk to a village, get a criminal, tie his hands and take him back to the police station without the interference of others. Today it takes an army to do the same job. The wars fractured the villages and made ethnicity a centralized and polarizing issue. The Pashtuns are hated in this part of the country. The Uzbek strongmen wanted to take Pashtun land by force and claimed that they didn't have any right to the land. Uzbek warlords, who were very poor men during the war, have become multi-millionaires after the war and people follow them blindly. It was the same when the Taliban were in power; they preferred the Pashtuns over the Uzbeks and Tajiks.

I found out from my brother that my nieces, children of my oldest brother who had passed away, were living in Maimana. I had met them once before in Peshawar, some time ago when I was taking my mother to the United States with me. My oldest brother had married again, a local girl from Maimana, after his first wife died. They had four kids, in addition to five kids from his first wife. The children from the first wife are in the United States, but those from the second wife live in Maimana. During the Soviet-Afghan war the oldest son was killed by the Mujahidin and his body was dumped in a well. His mother found him after a month or so and amazingly his body had not decomposed and she recognized him. The second son got hit with a rocket and lost his lower jaw, but is still alive. I went to his home and saw his beautiful kids. I wish I had the means to send him abroad for plastic surgery, but at that age even for public relation purposes nobody is going to touch him. A beautiful young Afghan girl married him even with the deformity of his wound. She treats her husband like a hero.

* * *

The ethnic groups in this part of Afghanistan, who lived in peace for a couple of centuries, now hate each other. After President Dawoud was assassinated and communists took over civil war started among the ethnic groups and each ethnic group committed atrocities against the others. I travelled with the Norwegian military unit to a valley called the Jailer Valley to meet the Pashtuns, who were causing the most problem in the province. When you pass by the villages the Uzbek villages are intact, but when the Uzbek warlord took over this area after allied forces got rid of the Taliban, all of the Pashtun villages were destroyed by the militia forces of the Uzbek warlords. The houses are all made out of mud and the only valuable materials in them were the ceiling rafters. In order to get those rafters the whole house had to be destroyed.

The residents of these villages abandoned their homes and either went to Herat, Iran or to Pakistan. The few that stayed live in poverty. The land which belonged to the Pashtuns was taken by force by Uzbek warlords or strong men. When any of them returned their land was in the hand of others. They filed claims but almost all the government employees are Uzbeks that would make the process slower; it takes years for a very legitimate case to be reviewed. The governance is so weak and corrupt that the residents, especially the Pashtuns, prefer to go to the shadow government of the Taliban for their disputes rather than the government. For most, the motive is not ideology—it's about immediate justice. The Taliban judge reaches a verdict the same day; there are witnesses in the shora (it is like a city council in the village) and the decision is made.

Nangy (in the middle) with two local leaders in northern Afghanistan

We stopped at a village to talk to people and find out what we could do to help them rebuild their village. The people were very reluctant to talk to anyone until I started talking to them in my very poor Pashto. I introduced myself as the late General Abdul Ghafar Khan's grandson and after that the whole environment changed. Most of them remembered from what their fathers or grandfathers told them that the land they now lived on was given to them by my grandfather. One old man came close to me and asked me if I was Abdullah Jan's son, and wanted to know where my brothers were. They all started calling me Sardar Sahib (a title given to all of Mohammadzai tribe, who were from the king's clan), and kept on saying that I was their cousin. I was amazed how much kinship means to these tribal people. My Norwegian friends who spent weeks in these villages couldn't get people to say a portion of what they told me. I became very popular among the Norwegian officers and they jokingly gave me the title of King of Faryab.

A tribal leader in a northern village in Faryab, who knew my grandfather

I remember when I went to these villages with the Norwegian military. At night we camped at the top of hills for security and dug trenches to sleep in. I have not seen so many stars in the sky, ever. Although at times when we slept outside it was very cold and sometimes snowed on us; I absolutely loved it. It reminded me of one time that my son-in-law invited me to go camping. I refused, saying that I wouldn't like to sleep on the ground and didn't think I would enjoy it. I proved myself totally wrong on these trips in Maimana. I could sleep on the ground and actually greatly enjoyed it.

Digging a trench on a hilltop in a northern tribal area

The Pashtun villages built in the border area between Turkmenistan and Afghanistan are divided among many clans: Shomolzai, Achekzai, Noorzai, Ali Zai, Ishaqzai, and others. Something that I didn't know was each village is an almost pure descendent of only one clan. For example, if you go to the village of Ghalbala everybody is from the Noorzai tribe and descendants of one father. The whole village is first, second and third cousins. If somebody else by chance moves to that village they are not accepted very well and are looked at as a foreigner. Sometimes these cousins separate from each other to make their own clan. Intermarriage is very common among Afghans and marrying a cousin is permissible in Muslim law. Owning a lot of land is very prestigious so the person who owns the most becomes the leader of that village.

The land they live on was 95% dry; there was no irrigation system to water the land. There are some springs but most of the land is watered only by rain. If there is a drought then everybody goes hungry. Where there is enough rain water for the land it is cultivated twice a year: wheat for the first season and in the second season melons and a plant

169

which they get oil from. In the second season of the year there is not even a drop of rain or water. Locals told me that those plants grow their roots so deep that the moisture of the ground keeps them alive and the melons are the best in the world. Most of these people were nomads and sheep herders and moved from these places to areas where there was grazing for their animals, especially during spring time where most of the hills were covered with greenery. Families pack a tent and children and camp on the grazing lands; living there for months at a time. Drinking water is a big problem, although the coalition forces are digging deep wells in these areas. Still there are villages that have no wells and no water. Young girls and women travel on their donkeys for five or more kilometers to bring water for their families.

Driving through the countryside of Maimana is beautiful, but very sad at times. You see children as young as eight years old, who spend all day being a shepherd, coming home with the herd at night. In one village I saw a school closed and converted to a stable for donkeys. I asked the village elder why it was not used for the purpose it was built. He answered that if they send their kids to school, who was going to attend to the herd which was the primary source of their survival? That left me speechless.

Almar is the capital of the district of the same name and is located approximately 20 miles from Maimana. My grandfather had some land there which was given to my aunt. When she died, according to Muslim law, her husband couldn't inherit it, so it came back to my father who was the eldest of the family, and my father sold the land when he was alive. I had never been there, but with the Norwegians and USAID I travelled to that city several times.

The first time we attended this large shora of the Ghalbala and Khwaja Ghawhar Pashtun elders. I introduced myself to the district governor and he immediately recognized the family name and stated that his family lived in a village next to Kariz Qala, where my brother lived. I sat next to this tall Pashtun from Ghalbala, and when I introduced myself to him, he introduced himself to me as the grandson of a Kochi (nomad) tribal leader. I remembered his name from the stories my father told me and he hugged me and said that his father told him that the land they own right now was given to them by my grandfather. He had a long, grayish beard and I thought he was close to my age, but he was much younger. We had discussions about redevelopment projects for their villages and security.

A gathering of local village elders and civil authorities

The Norwegian team bought a sheep to slaughter and cook for lunch. The chief of police and his crew did the slaughtering and cooking, but when it came lunch time, the district governor split the group. He took the Norwegians, the USAID, the USDA people and me to one room and all the Pashtuns went to another room. I asked where the Pashtuns were and he replied that he sent them to a different room. I got up and excused myself and went to their room and they were very happy to see me. They felt that they were discriminated against as Pashtuns because the district governor was an Uzbek. I don't think that it was done intentionally, but that was the perception of the Pashtuns. They even skipped tea after lunch, which is never done, to show the governor that they were upset. I was the only one to say goodbye to them when they left.

When I left, I saw a police officer enter a room and then shut its door. I asked the officer who was guarding the room what was going on. He said that yesterday they had captured a Talib and now he was interrogating him. I was very curious to see this Talib and talk to him. The chief of police allowed me to enter the room and talk to the captured man. The moment I saw him, he reminded me of the man I visited in Pomona Valley Hospital many years ago when the Mujahidin were fighting the Soviet forces. He was a small man, very dirty with torn clothes and a very long beard. He didn't speak Dari so I spoke to him in my broken Pashto and asked him what he did for a living. He responded that he was a shepherd. I asked why he was there. He said that he was tending his herd and some Talibs came toward him with the police chasing them. They escaped, but the policemen mistook him for a Talib. To me he didn't look any different from the people that I just had lunch with, but that is the biggest problem we have when fighting counter insurgency. Those, who cause problems, are from the people of that region and can hide within a village without any problem.

The next day, still in Almar, I saw a man running toward me. I recognized him from a shora I had attended. He told me that his herd had developed some disease and he desperately needed antibiotics to cure them. He wanted to know if I could ask the USDA to help him. I immediately told my friend from USDA about the problem, but he told me that it would take a month to process the paperwork. I told the man and he was very disappointed and wanted the medicine as fast as possible before his sheep began dying. I felt very sympathetic and I told him to come see me in Maimana and I would buy it for him out of my own pocket. He showed up the next day.

Next to the Almar police department and the governor's office was a health clinic run by Afghan doctors and funded through the department of health. The head of Faryab public health ministry took my hand and said, "Let's go to the clinic and you can see how desperate we are for any kind of assistance." I told him that I wasn't able to give direct aid but I could identify areas that needed help and suggest them to those I worked for and with that could provide aid.

A clinic in a northern village

The clinic was in a dilapidated mud building, no running water, no electricity, and only two real doctors: one maternity and the other a general practitioner. Four of the five nurses had no training. About 6,000 patients visit this clinic every month. It had one well but with a broken pump. They had to bring water in containers from the police department well which was across the street. The pump had been broken for months and there was no money for repairs. They showed me the well and begged me to fix it. I had this wonderful woman from the army who was in charge of the funds for the army reconstruction. She promised to take care of it, but unfortunately her assignment was finished and it took me two months to convince the man who replaced her. Finally the pump was fixed so the patients could have drinking water while waiting to be examined. The total cost of the pump and labor was $3,000 USD.

A local doctor celebrating the installation of a water pump to his clinic

My next trip to Almar we stayed at the police compound at night and in the morning went to the Ghalbala valley to look at the road and the villages on the way and find out what we could do to help the population. There were many villages in Ghalbala valley, a few of them populated by Uzbeks and Afghan Arabs. Afghan Arabs have lived in Afghanistan for centuries, probably dating back to when Islam first came to Afghanistan. They are not the Arabs who came recently to fight the Soviets and later joined Al Qaida. The rest of the villages were all occupied by Pashtuns.

We travelled for four hours and went only 22 kilometers. The roads were not actually roads; just good trails for donkeys and motorcycles. The dangers of travelling these roads are mostly from IED's. The roads are all dirt, and it is easy to dig a hole, put in an IED and cover it. When a car hit it, it would blow up. We didn't encounter any and when we arrived at our destination, were going to camp on top of this hill which had a view of the entire valley. In the car I was in, we had the district governor, the head of the public health, a USAID representative and my associate. As we were climbing the hill, at about 5.00PM local time, a barrage of machine gun fire and rockets started toward us from the hills across the valley. We didn't stop and kept driving to find cover. Once we stopped I got out of the car and rushed to an area where the insurgents couldn't see me. That was when the car I was in got hit in the driver side window. The car was armored and the rounds smashed the outside glass but couldn't penetrate. Bill, the driver, jumped out, ran and climbed the hill to safety. My friend and I who got out of the car remained behind the hill in cover and could hear the rockets and bullets pass over our heads making a woofing sound. We remained there for about half an hour and then a few more people joined us. We did not have communication with the rest of the convoy, they were all on top of the hill in good cover and we were at the base of the hill and still in danger. There were about five of us and I volunteered to climb the back side of the hill to let the rest know where we were. I climbed the side where the insurgents couldn't have a clear view of me. I got to the top where the rest of the convoy was but they couldn't do anything until dark and then went in Humvees with no lights on using night vision goggles and brought the rest to safety.

Before everybody was on top the Norwegian team started to return fire at the insurgents and it was very intense. This happened at the time when most of the wheat harvest was collected in mounds and the whole hillside caught on fire and burned probably 500 acres of harvest. We called in air support and B-1 bombers came over but left without doing anything other than probably taking photos. We were very upset, but then saw several Kochi tents around that area and knew they didn't drop any bombs for fear of hurting civilians. The firefight died down and we camped at the top of the hill that night and slept in trenches. A village leader who we had met before brought us soup and Afghan flat bread for dinner, which was much better than military rations.

The reasons for our trip to Ghalbala were many: to survey the road, to find a site for a clinic, to identify places to dig deep wells and to locate a site to build a police watch station. The road survey was done by a civil engineer from the US army as we travelled from village to village.

Our camp on a hilltop

Local young kids visiting the camp

To Lift a Mirror, for What You've Lost

The public health director had the responsibility of identifying the site for the clinic and deep wells. The Norwegian team was going to find the site for the police post, and this proved to be the hardest. We all thought that the hilltop was the best position for that because it was safe and had a clear view of the whole valley. The problem was that from the hilltop you could see very clearly into the village elder's compound and others, as well. This was a problem because Afghans don't want anybody to look inside their homes. Even guests come and sit in the outside part of the compound. Only very close male relatives are allowed to see their women. So we had to negotiate this with the village leader.

The village elder came to the hilltop in the morning with a pot of tea and bread and tentatively approved our plan, but insisted that we build the observation post so that it did not look directly at his compound and we agreed. More people came to us to claim we burned their harvest and wanted money, but we refused to pay them, because they allowed the insurgents to fire at us from their land. Later in the morning of that day we went back to the village elder's home for a gathering of the village residents. We discussed our plans for the clinic, the deep wells and police post with them and had tea and bread (with thick fresh cream which was just made). The team commander made a speech and thanked them for their hospitality. The last thing the commander of the team told them was, "We are here to bring peace to you, and we want to help you. We are not here to fight. The moment peace arrives we are on our way back to our families."

We travelled to our next shora in Khwaja Gawhar valley, where another village elder and power broker was in charge. This man was a warlord who had changed sides many times, mostly to maintain status and power, but above all for survival. It's important here that I share with you something that many westerners do not realize. The Taliban is made up of several different groups:

- There are hard core Talibs who are connected to Al Qaida, and their agenda is to fight the west anyway they can.

177

- There are Talibs who perceive the west as invaders who are trying to change the Afghan and Muslim way of life and to exploit the riches of the invaded country for their self-interest.

- There are Talibs who are connected with the insurgent groups in Pakistan and work with the ISI and Haqqanni group from the Khyber pakhtunkhaw area. And the ones connected with the Quetta shora headed by Mullah Omar

- And there are Talibs who are not actually Talib by ideology, but because of necessity or grief. Necessity because the Talib leaders pay these people to intimidate others at night, to shoot at policemen or at a convoy or terrorize a village for money. And grief, because they are not listened to. They have land disputes; their land was taken by powerful warlords that control the government and they get nothing by way of compensation or justice so they turn to the Taliban.

A local warlord who joined the local police

At the village of Khwaja Gawhar, we had a shora at the village elder's house. The district governor pointed two guys out to me and said they were both Talibs, but he couldn't do anything about it. The village elder had a connection with Karzai's government. As a matter of fact, rumors

178

were that Karzai gave him $100,000 Afghanis ($2,000.00 dollars) and a Toyota to buy the vote of his entire village during presidential elections. He was from the Shomolzai tribe that came here from Ghazni province many years ago. His father was a feudal lord who had his own soldiers (and prison). My grandfather gave him land as well.

Meeting with the local village elders

One time the Military Observation Team commanders responsible for that part of Faryab district asked me to go with them and I was very glad to. Spring had come and the hills of Maimana were covered with a green blanket of wild grass and later the wild tulips would show up. There was absolutely no dust in the air and it was the cleanest you'd breathe anywhere but the mud on the so called roads was intolerable. At times the vehicles were not able make it alone so we towed one another as we each took turns in getting buried in the mud.

We reached a place called Russian Hill, (named so because when Russians occupied the country they had installed a couple of cannons

179

on top of this hill) located in a Pashtun area that was considered dangerous. We camped and dug trenches to sleep in. The commander ordered the interpreter to go and buy a sheep, which was slaughtered (I helped him cut the meat) and cooked. The interpreter made the most delicious Northern rice pilaf with sheep meat.

A typical rural road in northern Afghanistan during rainy season

A sheep is slaughtered by local police for us on the hill top

After dinner we all sat around and the commander took his iPod out and played some music. He jokingly warned us that we better like the music and not say anything bad about it. The music was from a Norwegian artist, but she was singing in English. The music was actually wonderful; to my taste, very soft and meaningful. We told him that we liked it, he replied, "Good, because that's my wife." She was a recording artist and during the Norwegian Independence Day she would come to Maimana and entertain us. What touched and honored me was that before she started to sing one song, she said, "I'm dedicating this song to a very special man who has left his family to help bring peace to his place of birth and that is Nangy." I recently received an e-mail from the commander and he said that his wife just finished recording the songs that she sang for us.

We went again to Ghalbala and from there to Khwaja Gawhar and back to Almar from another direction. The roads were again very hard to travel and many places were washed out during the flood. Since the terrain in this area was just top soil and no rocks, during the rainy season the trails are washed away very easily. We crossed these roads without problem, but it was very time consuming until we reached a gravel road.

Our car also had the governor and at a point where the road curved to the left I saw a motorcycle about 50 yards ahead and its two passengers on the side of the road. When we got closer one of the guys by the motorcycle made eye contact with me. At the same time, the governor looked at him and told Steve, who was driving, to stop the car because the governor was suspicious of that man. Bill couldn't hear and the two got on the motorcycle and drove to the opposite side. Then we saw another motorcycle with a man and a woman, her face turned to the other side as we passed them.

We were driving without worry; the convoy was arranged in a way where we had two military cars with weapons in front, then two civilian cars, mine and the governor's car with his body guards, and further behind us the last military vehicle. We turned the curve and saw a truck parked on the side of the road. The officer in the front car did a radio check with all of us and everybody answered except the last vehicle. The officer called three times. No answer. We were all ordered to stop so he could turn around and check if everything was okay. We stopped on the side of the road and waited until one of the soldiers came to our car with the saddest face and told us the vehicle behind us was hit by a roadside bomb. All four passengers were dead; four Norwegian soldiers, one of them a Lieutenant Colonel named Tron. We called for a medevac (medical evacuation) helicopter to come for the bodies.

I was close to Lieutenant Colonel Tron and had many conversations with him in the dining room back at camp. He liked Afghanistan so much that he suggested to a friend of his to volunteer for a tour of duty in Afghanistan. His friend volunteered, but an unfortunate incident happened. He was shot and paralyzed. Tron felt terrible for his friend and came back to Afghanistan to finish his friend's remaining days of his tour. He was the one who, in every shora, would say that we were there to bring peace to Afghanistan, we were not there to kill anyone. He would have finished his friend's tour in just two more weeks, but now he was dead.

We came to the conclusion that the roadside bomb was set by the motorcycle drivers and the motorcycle with a woman was not really a woman but a man in a burqa (face cover, Afghan style) to fool us. The truck on the road was there to warn the insurgents if anybody came while they were setting the bomb. That truck was driven by three young teenagers; who were taken to the police station but we didn't have any evidence that they were part of the insurgency.

The blast from the IED was so strong that pieces of the car flew about 100 feet up the hill next to the road and burned the entire hillside. After calling in the medevac we got a call from another unit that a group of about 30 insurgents were moving toward our position. We all climbed the hill to our right and dug trenches to wait in until reinforcements came, which took a long time. The quick reaction force arrived but the insurgents didn't show. Still we were stuck on top of the hill for 12 hours until all the debris from the blown up vehicle was completely recovered and then we drove back to camp.

Our next trip was again to Ghalbala. This time in a convoy of many cars and with bomb sniffing dogs. We traveled with the PRT commander to meet the village elder of Ghalbala to distribute mosquito nets to the residents of the valley and to check the sick and give them medicine. The trip went very slowly. We stopped at one village which had been very friendly the previous visits but this time the residents told us to please leave immediately. I conveyed the message to the commander and we left.

The roads were very bad and we were not taking any chances; making new trails, not using the old ones, because of the road side bombs. It took us a very long time to reach our destination. The team commander decided to stop in a village just before Ghalbala and asked me to talk to the villagers to see if it was okay to camp there. I told them while we were there we would examine their sick and distribute mosquito nets. They had seen me before in shoras and one of them came close to me and said, "Cousin you are welcome to stay, but be careful." I didn't think anything of it and we started setting up camp.

My friend from USAID came over and asked me if we should call the Ghalbala village elder and tell him that we were camping in this village rather than driving the rest of the way. I didn't think it was a good idea. But somebody else from the village must have called him because in an hour he showed up with food for the Afghan's with us to break their fast (it was the month of Ramadan) and some blankets and cushions for the Afghan doctors who were travelling with us. He was in a rush and left everything for us to distribute. Before leaving he cornered me and said, "Be very careful, tonight you will be shot at. Be careful." When he left, I went to the commander's tent and told him what the village elder had told me.

The camp was arranged with the military vehicles on the outside and the civilian vehicles in the middle and the surrounding hills were occupied by our protection forces. The only hill that we didn't cover was about three kilometers away and we judged it not a danger. By 9.00PM everybody who was not on watch went to their cots and fell asleep. I was awake because of my restless leg syndrome. (My calves start hurting the moment I go to bed, so I sit on my bed with my legs crossed for about an hour or so until I'm really tired then I go to sleep sitting up.)

At exactly 10.00PM from the hill in front of us came a barrage of rockets and machinegun fire with tracer bullets. Our protection force was ready and responded immediately. We could see the bullets pass overhead and hit the hillside behind us. The people who were asleep woke up and ran for cover. My bed was just behind the armored car that was assigned to me and I had my armored vest inside the car. The civilian Afghan doctors next to me woke up in a panic and ran to my car. One of them put on my armored vest and sat in my seat, the rest piled in next to him. I and my associate, who was responsible for my safety, were left outside for the whole firefight. The fire fight went on for about forty minutes and then stopped. We stayed up all night to be ready just in case there was more incoming fire, but nothing happened.

In the morning the commander was very mad. He asked me if we should call the Ghalbala leader to find out why he didn't tell us way ahead of time about the insurgents' intentions and how he knew that we were going to be shot at. If he didn't cooperate, we would cut off work on all the projects in his village. The village leader did come in the morning and the commander and a few of us went to talk to him. After the commander threatened him he requested that he talk to just the commander and me. The commander agreed and everybody else left. The leader stated that he knew who shot at us and last night in the firefight. The man was injured with three others and two others were killed. He said that the people who shot at us were not from his clan, but came from other places. As far as development projects in his village, he didn't care if we did any. He said, "We lived like this for the last 30 years and we are used to it, and besides, what have you accomplished so far?" He was right; we had not done much in that area.

He left and that night came back with some wonderful lamb stew, breads and tea for us. He cornered me again and said sleep well... tonight nobody is going to shoot at you. He was right nobody did.

The truth of the matter is that the insurgents are a part of these villages and probably brothers, cousins, or other relations. The elders, even if they don't agree with the insurgents, won't give them away for the following three major reasons:

First they are kin. Even if they don't agree, they won't give them away because it is against their code of *Pakhtunwali*.

Second, they are not sure how they could defend themselves if they gave away information on the insurgents. There would be reprisals and coalition forces are not there 24 hours a day to help them and they don't have any weapons to defend themselves.

Third, what would happen if the insurgents win and the coalition loses? They live in this country and we do not. Again, there would be reprisals against all who helped the coalition.

Something that everyone must understand about most of the people in Afghanistan; their every decision and action was based on survival. The population is trying to survive in all circumstances and that is the way Pashtuns have always operated.

We broke camp the next day headed back to Almar and then Maimana, being just as careful as we had previously to avoid roadside bombs. About 15 kilometers from Almar, we came under fire from some hills around us. We all stopped and hid behind our armored vehicles and let the military take care of it. It didn't last long. The insurgents left the area as soon as the Norwegians started firing back.

* * *

From the beginning of my tour I allocated some of my money for charity for needy Afghans. In Maimana one day I passed a row of bread sellers on the side of the street. Northern flat bread is my favorite and I wanted to buy some and munch on it as I was going to pick up the handmade pocket knives I ordered for my son, son-in-law and myself. (The master knife maker, who was making them for me was very old and taught the trade to his sons and grandsons, claimed that the knives were made out of the steel from destroyed Russian tanks. He told me a story that once when a Talib was captured and searched, he had this wonderful handmade knife in his pocket. The soldier asked the man where he got the knife and was told about the master knife maker. The soldier was so impressed that he ordered two knives from him to supposedly give one to President Bush and one to Vice President Cheney.)

The young bread sellers of Maimana

The bread sellers were all girls nine or ten years old, and one woman. I bought bread from this girl who couldn't be more than nine years old, and probably weighed not more than 50 lbs. I wanted to take a picture of her, but she turned her face and objected saying, "Don't! My father will get mad at me, please don't." I understood and didn't take her picture (I did take some pictures, from the crowd anyways.) I bought all the breads from all of the kids, which came to not more than a few hundred dollars, and told them and the woman to give it to all the people around them as a gift. There were probably about two thousand flat breads and they were all gone in a matter of an hour or so.

As I walked away, the thought came to me what an unjust world we have. These young girls are robbed of their childhood and then when they get to the age of puberty, they are practically sold to the highest bidder. And most of the time to an old man. Looking at those innocent, young, beautiful children and seeing their future in my mind turned my bright day to a dark and bleak night. I didn't know who to blame: religion, tradition, poverty, exploitation of the masses by warlords, ineffective government or lack of education. Or was it the foreign powers that should be blamed who have come to this ancient land and are trying to change the old tradition and way of life of these people in the name of democracy and modernization but the real objective is to find raw mineral resources to exploit, and create more markets for their goods. To keep these neighbors fighting each other and thus selling war equipment to both sides for profit. Or maybe all of that is part of why things are the way they are.

When you impartially judge things, what choice did the west, especially the US, have after 9/11? The United States, on the other side of the world, was attacked by Al Qaeda fundamentalists and their attack was planned in Afghanistan. The Taliban leadership was approached and asked to hand over Bin Laden—he's what the US wanted—not a war in Afghanistan. But because of the Afghan tradition of *pakhtuwali,* he was given safe haven and so the Afghan people bear the brunt of being caught between the two. Their way of life so different from that of the west it can scarcely be comprehended by those who never have experienced it or are no longer tied to it.

Regardless—my heart goes out to the children for their lost childhood and the never to be seen or realized opportunities for these young girls.

CHAPTER NINETEEN
Trip to Ghormach

One Song (by Rumi)
Translated by Coleman Barks

Every war and every conflict between human beings
has happened because of some disagreement about
names.

It is such an unnecessary foolishness,
because just beyond the arguing
there is a long table of companionship
set and waiting for us to sit down.

What is praised is one, so the praise is one too,
many jugs being poured into a huge basin.
All religions, all this singing, one song.
The differences are just illusion and vanity.
Sunlight looks a little different on this wall
than it does on that wall
and a lot different on this other one,
but it is still one light.

We have borrowed these clothes,
these time-and-space personalities,
from a light, and when we praise,
we are pouring them back in.

Ghormach is a district of Badghis province which is now governed by
the governor of Faryab (for security and operation reasons). My whole
trip to Afghanistan would not have been complete, if I did not go on
this trip. I experienced the war from the eyes of our young brave

soldiers who have put their lives in danger in order to bring peace to the Afghans (as well as to the world). At the same time, my respect goes out to those patriotic Afghans who are misguided by a few warlords who have used religion and nationalism for their own self-interest. They fight for what they believe is right for their country.

I was sent to Ghormach to help with an army group who had taken a tactical radio station there and wanted to find out if the radio station could help the coalition forces reach the populace—getting news and information directly to the people. At the same time a group of American military doctors were visiting Ghormach to treat the sick and improve relations with the people as part of the COIN (counter insurgency) concept; they thought that I could be of some help to them. We got up at 5.00AM at camp Marmal and were picked up by a Blackhawk helicopter for the trip to Ghormach making one stop along the way. The flight time was not long, it took us about 1 hr. 45 minutes to reach the FOB (Forward Operating Base). Its landing zone was inside the FOB perimeter and we were greeted by our friends when we landed.

The FOB was occupied by an American and Norwegian Army units as instructors for the ANA (Afghan National Army). The facilities were very basic. Tents for everything: offices, dining room, sleeping, and so on. Bathrooms were like outhouses, and water was not available except for what was trucked in. The Navy was trying to dig a deep well when I was there and had gone as deep as 730 feet, but had not hit a water source. There was a truck with a water tank for all the soldiers to use buckets to draw water to wash their face, brush their teeth or take a shower. (To shower, you filled a tank with water, put it on a shelf, and then tilted it into a gutter and you stood under the gutter as the water came out). Breakfast was served from early in the morning till about 8.00AM and was coffee, bacon, hush puppies and sometimes bread. Lunch was either MREs or chicken nuggets and onion rings or French fries. Dinner was rice, chicken nuggets and some other kind of meat.

On one side of the FOB there were two bunker shelters (bunker shelters had a roof and walls made of concrete). These were used when the insurgents fired rockets at the FOB (tents were not very good protection). This happened at night twice while I was there. The biggest fear was IEDs. While I was there, three IEDs went off. One of them destroyed a police car and injured the occupants. One was wounded very seriously and they called in a medevac from Maimana for him.

One evening about 10.00PM a barrage of rockets came toward our camp from the hills. Most passed overhead and a few hit around the camp. The Afghan Army personnel responded by firing back with their antique cannons as we went to our assigned bunkers. All of our young soldiers in the bunker demonstrated the highest level of bravery. I did not see one soldier scared. They all joked and laughed until we got the "all clear" and were allowed to go back to our tents and go to sleep.

In the morning I visited the commander of the Afghan Army unit and asked him about the shooting the night before. I wanted to know the effectiveness of their cannon fire and how they knew where to aim. The commander was very honest; he stated that they had no idea where the fire was coming from. They fired their cannons just to show the people of the village they were responding to being attacked. He also said the people who fired the rockets likely were not close to their weapons. They were probably drinking tea below the hills and fired the rockets by remote control.

The people of Ghormach were much different than those in the other parts of Faryab I had been in. They were bigger with long beards. Tall and rough looking, they weren't very friendly and looked at us suspiciously. Even the kids were not very approachable. We offered a few of the kids some apple jam we had with us and even though I had traditional Afghan clothes on they threw the jam away and would not let me take their pictures. I could not wait to talk to someone with my broken Pashto, so I stopped at a shop where a group of tall Afghans were standing around. I greeted one Afghan with a long grey beard who was probably younger than me but appeared to be older and asked him about the harvest. He responded that it was better than the year before. Then I asked him were there any poppy fields in Ghormach. He answered yes, without any fear or change of facial expression, but added that a lot of people did not grow poppy this year because the price was very low (only 2,000 Afg. per kilogram), so people have changed to Saffron. I did not know the real reason for less growth of poppy. Was it only economic or because the Taliban controls almost all of Ghormach? When the Taliban were in power the poppy growth in the country was almost zero.

A local merchant in Ghormach

The most surprising thing to me was the morale of the Pashtun population. In other parts of the Faryab province, where I met different ethnic groups, they tended to try and be accommodating. But most of them looked at us with caution: kids would not approach us and would often run away. In Ghormach, kids would not run away. They would stop and examine us without fear and would not do what we asked them to do.

Ghormach is all Pashtun from three clans: Achekzai, Zamanzai, and Tokhi, and a very small group of Musazais. Achekzais and Zamanzais are a branch of Durrani tribe and the Tokhis are a branch of the Ghelzai tribe. Like other provinces and local governments Ghormach has a shadow governor who nominates his own administration and applies Sharia (law), which has been in practice in the district for a few years. The Government has no connection with the villages and the villagers do not have any services available to them. There are approximately 160 villages in the Ghormach district, including the bazaar.

For the sick, there was a clinic in the bazaar, which was built when Dawoud Khan was the president of the county. It had two doctors, one male and one female, one male nurse and two other nurses who are not really nurses, but untrained workers. I learned that a female nurse had a fight with the female doctor and quit six months ago and had not been replaced. The clinic did not have electricity or running water (there were two hand pumps in two wells but one pump was broken). The head doctor told me that he treats 3,200-3,500 patients a month, but they cannot perform surgery because both doctors are only general practitioners.

So in my native land, the government existed, to a degree, but failed (or neglected) to be a means to help the people it governed. This is something I thought about a great deal on the many nights I was away from my family and my home in the United States.

CHAPTER TWENTY
Coming home
(and final thoughts)

Time to go Home (by Rumi)
Translated by Coleman Barks

Late and starting to rain,
it's time to go home.
We've wandered long enough
in empty buildings.
I know it's tempting to stay
and meet those new people.
I know it's even more sensible
to spend the night here with them,
but I want to go home.

We've seen enough beautiful places
with signs on them saying
This is God's House. That's seeing the
grain like the ants do,
without the work of harvesting.
Let's leave grazing to cows and go
where we know what everyone really intends,
where we can walk around without clothes on.

I asked my wife to give me her honest opinion about my idea of writing this book. She told me I was such a lucky man; something she had learned all these years living with and listening to me. That I always followed my dream and somehow I succeeded in accomplishing it. Whether it was to abandon all I had back in Afghanistan and test my ability to make my life on my own, start a business without having any funds for it, or pursue a doctorate degree at one of the colleges in

Claremont, fly as a corporate pilot or to help my country of birth in a position where I could make a difference.

She told me why stop there. Why not finish the goal of writing this book. If nothing else comes out of it, it will be something I could leave my family and their family and friends. I was so discouraged at one time when I was struggling with the enormous changes that came to my life. Returning from Afghanistan, observing the simplicity of life, the actual material need that a person requires to live compared to the luxuries that I pursued or sought to acquire here in the United States. My wife would argue with me that I am not the same person she knew before I went back to Afghanistan. She would say that I have changed. I would not admit it then but she was right.

I thought about the experiences I had in Afghanistan. Her answer to my question gave me strength and direction, although I am not as young as I used to be, and do not have as much energy; her opinion made me rethink my priorities in life.

So I think this book is important—if only to share some things that would not be known if I don't get them down on paper. But I also believe it's important to share observations, based in my own experiences and knowledge, on what's going on in the country of my birth and how the country I chose to live and raise my family in can perhaps do a better job doing what it has since its inception—and that's try to help others even in faraway lands.

The situation in Afghanistan is so complex that most experts don't have a clear plan on how to deal with it. Some of the issues at hand:

- The Afghanistan illiteracy rate is probably higher than any other country in the world
- Afghanistan is also probably the poorest country in the world
- Afghanistan is also the most fractured society as far as ethnicity goes

- During the Russian invasion, all of the ethnic groups were armed
- The ethnic groups are homogenous in different parts of the country
- There are minorities in each homogenous areas
- Ethnic groups are controlled and supported by warlords
- Warlords are supported by neighboring countries and/or by coalition forces
- The Afghan government is weak, nonfunctional, and extremely corrupt.
- When Afghans feel that a foreign power has invaded the country, all ethnic groups unite for the cause. Not necessarily under one unified command but as separate groups, and that makes it very difficult for the perceived invaders to fight the Afghans.

As far as military campaigns and trade, Afghanistan has always been a crossroads. If we go back to the Great Game era; at that time this land was very important as a buffer between the two Imperial powers of Great Britain and Russia. The British and Russian governments paid much attention to this part of the world to defend their colonies in the countries neighboring Afghanistan.

After World War II, the United States replaced Great Britain, and the Soviet Union replaced Czarist Russia. The United States created several defensive pacts around the Soviet Union and its satellite countries. In south central Asia it was the Central Treat Organization (CENTO) both of Afghanistan's neighbors (Pakistan and Iran) became members of that pact. Afghanistan's neutrality benefitted the west, and the monarchy in Afghanistan was also in the west's advantage because they were anti-communist. But the balance of power has changed tremendously, with Pakistan and Iran becoming very powerful with modern American weapons, while Afghanistan still had airplanes with cloth wings and World War I weapons. Afghanistan requested weapons from the United States, but the US refused. President Eisenhower felt that Afghanistan was not an area of national interest, while Pakistan was. I assume the reason Eisenhower didn't sell weapons was because he didn't want to provoke the Soviets and besides the anti-communist monarchy was a hedge that the Soviets would not be able exercise any significant level of influence in Afghanistan.

But this backfired on the US. The new young, patriotic, Prime Minister of Afghanistan, Mohammad Dawoud, with the permission of the king requested weapons from the Soviet Union, which was supposed to have no strings attached. Of course that was not true. By refusing to sell military hardware to Afghanistan, the United States forced the Afghan government to become a client of the Soviets. This was the first mistake the US made. The monarchy didn't have any other choice but to commit their own biggest mistake; harming the future of Afghanistan by buying weapons from the Soviets (thus allowing the Soviets to influence the Afghan elite and military power structure).

Hundreds and hundreds of young Afghans, including young military officers, were part of the bargain to be educated in the Soviet Union. I was one of them. The young and elite of most developing nations, when observing the advance of other nations in all aspects of life, want to have the same in their own nation. The first scapegoat for their underdevelopment is the system of their government, which most of the time is true. They want to change the system through revolution, which they perceive to be faster, rather than evolution, a much slower process. For the Afghans who were indoctrinated by the Soviets, the Soviet model was adapted.

- The presence and strength of Taliban is a reality in Afghanistan.
- The majority of Afghans, share culture, religion and kinship with the Taliban, especially in the rural area. Although the majority of Afghans do not want to return to the Taliban era.

The Afghan population has four major ethnic groups, Pashtuns, Tajeks, Uzbeks and Hazaras. There are other minority groups such as Turkmens, Baluchis, Nooristani, Aimaqs, Arabs and some others. Pashtuns are the majority and have been the rulers of the country for almost two and a half centuries. The Pashtun monarchies have ruled the country with an iron fist and at times barbarically, but brought this country to a point where the Pashtun rulers were accepted by all other ethnic Afghans either through coercion or persuasion until the Soviet invasion of Afghanistan.

The Afghans fought the Soviets not under one unified command but in separate groups. Each group was identified by ethnicity, for example the Uzbeks fought under an Uzbek leader, the Tajeks under a Tajek leader and so on. They fought effectively. When the Soviets were defeated and left Afghanistan, the wartime leaders did not want to relinquish power to the central government for two reasons: there was no effective central government with an army and police to enforce the rule of law and second the leaders would not allow another ethnic group beside themselves to become the leader of the nation. The end result was that each leader became independent in their own area of influence and some even printed money in their own name as an independent nation. Afghanistan ceased to be a nation state under any semblance of the rule of law. The country was divided among the warlords and each one in their turn committed atrocities. One could not travel from one city to another unless he paid a toll.

Following the Soviet withdrawal from Afghanistan in 1989 and the collapse of Najibullah's Soviet-backed regime in 1992, the country fell into chaos as various Mujahidin factions fought for control. Mullah Omar started his movement with less than 50 armed madrasah students, known simply as the Taliban (Students). His recruits came from madrasahs in Afghanistan and from the Afghan refugee camps across the border in Pakistan. They fought against the rampant corruption that had emerged in the civil war period and were initially welcomed by Afghans weary of warlord rule. Reportedly, in early 1994, Omar led 30 men armed with 16 rifles to free youths who had been kidnapped and raped by a warlord, hanging the local commander from a tank gun barrel. His movement gained momentum through the year, and he quickly gathered recruits from Islamic schools. By November 1994, Omar's movement managed to capture the whole of Kandahar Province and then captured Herat in September

1995. Mullah Omar and his followers captured about 90% of the country. Once they had control and Bin Laden joined them, they became just like the other warlords, and committed crimes against other ethnic Afghans and practiced an extreme version of Islam which the Afghans were not familiar with.

After 9/11, the United States with the Northern Alliance (an alliance among Tajeks, Uzbeks and Hazara's) invaded Afghanistan, and got rid of the Taliban. Now the real dilemma started. What kind of government should the west bring to the Afghan people to make everybody happy?

The west decided that the King should be brought back as a symbol of unity. A Pashtun from the same clan as the King become the president and the Tajeks, Uzbeks and Hazarras were given other positions in the government. The perception was that the Pashtuns would be happy that the King remained as a symbol, and a Pashtun became the President. The other ethnic Afghans should be happy that they ended up with the powerful positions of Defense Minister, Minister of Interior and so on.

In my judgment, the west made the following mistakes:

- Monarchy was the only solid infrastructure in Afghanistan, most of the rural Afghans identified with it. Establishing a republic was premature
- In a country where illiteracy is more than 90%, how could ordinary citizen understand the importance of voting. The warlords legitimize themselves by buying votes by thousands.
- The west was shortsighted by keeping the warlords who committed crimes against humanity in power (we even support them still today). If we could defeat the Taliban, we could have controlled these other groups very easily, especially at a time when all the neighboring countries were with us to fight against terrorism. Even now that a central government is formed and it is working to build a strong army and police force for the Afghan government, we still support the warlords

who don't want peace for Afghanistan because they would lose power and financial gain.

Another development after the Soviets left the country; the neighboring nations around Afghanistan became engaged in the internal affairs of Afghanistan for their own reasons.

Let's start with Pakistan (who has many motives in Afghanistan):

1- Perception of closer ties of the Afghan government with India. Thus if a war breaks out between India and Pakistan, Pakistan would not have to fight on two fronts.
2- Perception of losing the Khyber Pashtunkhaw (formerly called the North-West Frontier) part of the disputed territory between Afghanistan and Pakistan.
3- Tremendous economic loss if the Afghanistan government is not friendly with Pakistan. Pakistani products are in abundance in Afghan markets.
4- Trade with the central republics of the former Soviet Union via Afghanistan, and getting the natural gas of Turkmenistan to Pakistan through Afghanistan. Therefore Pakistan wants the future government in Afghanistan to be under the influence of Pakistan. And so far, Pakistan has control of the Taliban and religious insurgent groups under a false banner of Islam.

The problems between Afghanistan and Pakistan have roots in the Durand treaty, where the majority of Pashtuns were separated from the mainland. I would like to shed some light on this issue since I believe that this unrecognized border is the basis of disagreement between Afghanistan and Pakistan.

The Durand agreement backfired

There are several reasons why the British Empire drew the Durand line and separated the Afghan tribes:

- To divide the Afghans and thus be better able to control the tribes.

- To control the strategic Khyber Pass that most of the invaders especially the Afghans used to invade India.
- To create a buffer to prevent any possible Russian invasion of India.
- Although the British Empire could not stop the Pashtuns from crossing the border to join their relatives in either side of the border. By bribing the tribal chiefs and allowing them to have freedom within their tribal territories the British isolated the tribal area from making trouble for them and it worked for almost a century or more.
- When India was divided, and the new nation of Pakistan was created, the Pashtuns were not given the chance to decide on their future whether to join Pakistan, be an independent nation or join Afghanistan. The Afghan government wanted to have the Pashtuns on the other side of the Durand Line rejoin their relatives on the Afghanistan side. Pakistan did not like the idea. Although some of the past presidents and important political leaders of Pakistan were Pashtuns, the common people that were Pashtun wanted to join with Afghanistan. Pakistan started a crackdown on the leadership of the Pashtuns and arrested Khan Abdul Ghafar Khan who is also known as the frontier Gandhi and put him in jail for many years. When Khan Abdul Ghafrar Khan passed away in 1988, his wishes were to be buried in Afghanistan in the city of Jalalabad as a symbolic returning home.

The Durand Line was demarcated by the British and signed into a treaty in 1893 with the Afghan ruler Amir Abdur Rehman Khan through coercion. The treaty was to stay in force for a 100-year period.

- This disputed land was legally to be returned to Afghanistan in 1993 after the 100 year old Durand Treaty expired, similar to how Hong Kong was returned to China. Kabul has refused to renew the Durand Line treaty since it expired, Pakistan has tried to get Afghan warlords and the Taliban to sign a renewal contract of the Treaty, but not even the Taliban regime which was a product of Pakistan signed a renewal or agreed with the legitimacy of the treaty after its expiration.

- The Soviet invasion of Afghanistan made a lot of Pashtuns refugees. Most went to the other side of the border and were welcomed by their blood brothers, thus once again the Pashtuns became close. The Pakistani government not only tolerated it but encouraged the situation to build a fighting guerrilla force to use against the Soviets.
- Millions of Afghans, mostly Pashtuns, crossed the border and filled the refugee camps in the northwest frontier and Baluchistan areas of Pakistan.
- Once the Russians were defeated and left Afghanistan and the Mujahidin took control civil war started along ethnic lines in Afghanistan.
- The creation of Taliban among the Pashtuns had its base of support in tribal areas of Pakistan and the backing of the ISI (Pakistan's intelligence service).
- This union brought the Pashtuns closer on both sides of the border.
- When the northern alliance took control of Kabul with the help of the coalition forces after 9/11 that brought the Pashtuns even closer. The Pashtuns on both side of the border started the guerrilla war against the Tajek government in Kabul against the west and Pakistan.
- Today the Haqqani network which is the most active group of insurgents is based in North Waziristan, and Mullah Omar or the Quetta shora is based in the city of Quetta in Baluchistan.
- With a total population of 40 million on both sides of the border, and the spread of Pashtuns and their status all over Pakistan and Afghanistan, this has worried not only both of the countries but the west as well.
- Pakistan's fear of the Pashtuns as a nation by themselves is a big concern. Baluchistan which is a tribe of the Pashtuns, is another fear of Pakistan. If the situation in Afghanistan is not

brought under control both of these could impact the stability of the region.

- Pakistan could be divided again, and the Pashtuns in the Afghanistan side join the Pashtuns of Pakistan. About three million Pashtuns live in the north of Afghanistan, where the majority of the population is Tajeks and Uzbeks. There are intermarriages all over the country. Kabul is totally mixed and other ethnic groups are not numerous enough by themselves to take control. The Pashtuns would again be the majority.

- I believe that there is a resemblance between the Berlin wall and the Durand imaginary wall. There was no doubt IF the Berlin wall was going to crumble but rather when it would fall. The same question applies to the land of the Pashtuns.

Some of the other international players and their motives (that impact Afghanistan's ability for self-government and self-determination:

Iran:

Wouldn't like to have a conservative Sunni leadership to potentially join with Saudi Arabia.

Russia:

Does not want a conservative Muslim nation next to its southern Muslim nations to be radicalized by Afghans.

China:

China does not want a conservative Muslim nation next to its volatile Muslim population.

About Bringing Peace to Afghanistan

Afghanistan won't be able to have peace until the so called Taliban is integrated into society. All of this wouldn't have happened if a proven and legitimate system of government had been put back in power that had an identity and legitimacy among all Afghans. Now that the genie is out of the bottle and the king cannot be brought back to power from the grave. What are the options?

Things that cannot bring stability and peace to Afghanistan are:

- An ethnic divide is not going to bring peace, but would only bring more fighting and displacement of millions of people. Since no area could survive by itself, economically or militarily, they have to have other countries that identify with their ethnic roots in their regions, which further destabilizes the region.
- The west cannot bring peace militarily or by introducing their ideals and system of government and democracy.
- The cultural roots of this nation are very deep. The west cannot change it overnight or maybe not ever, because they are imported and not home grown. If the people don't see the need for it themselves, they resist the change.
- The west can start a dialog with the neighboring nations, and not interfere with the internal affairs of Afghanistan. The British Government during the late 19th century, after being defeated by the Afghans, did the same thing and was successful. Let the Afghans do what is necessary to bring unity to their country.

What are the essential elements to bring peace to Afghanistan?

- In a developed society a leader is elected not according to ethnicity but personal qualifications. In developing nations, it will take time to reach that ideal. Therefore the government of Afghanistan must remain with Pashtun majority with equal rights for the other ethnic groups.
- Pashtuns have ruled Afghanistan for more than three centuries. Being a traditional society with another 23 million Pashtuns on the other side of the border, Pashtuns right or wrong will not accept the rule of other ethnic groups until real home grown democracy is established.

- Improving the economy of the country and providing jobs.
- Educating the younger generation and children.
- Not interfering in cultural or religious affairs of the Afghans.
- Afghans are not ready for a federalist system unless the warlord mentality and strong man rule is eliminated.
- Strong governance with strong security forces. A legitimate government which can practice and enforce the rule of law.
- I believe the Afghan National Army should be built with a compulsory draft system, where every young citizen of Afghanistan of all ethnicities, should serve not for money alone but as a patriotic duty. While they are in service, they can be educated and taught national pride and unity.
- Minimizing corruption.
- Strong defense system to maintain the balance of power among the neighbors,
- International security forces must not leave the country, but remain in Afghanistan to be a deterrent against emergence of another insurgency.
- Coalition forces should stop mingling in internal affairs of Afghanistan.
- Emergence of a home grown leadership from the masses of Afghanistan without the interference of the coalition forces.
- Coalition forces must cease helping and giving millions of dollars of aid to the warlords.
- Some kind of arrangement must be made to resolve the border issue between Afghanistan and Pakistan.

The west (especially the United States), Saudi Arabia, and Israel must find a way to normalize relations with Iran. As long as Iran is kept isolated and intimidated, they will cause problems across the border in Afghanistan and be a headache for America and its allies.

I believe the best exit strategy would be to have a dialog with the Afghan neighbors, and convince them to stay out of Afghan internal affairs, and then let the Afghans do what they have always done. An emerging leader will rise and unite the country, and if they are not assisted by any other nations, their goals will be the Afghan goal.

In the name of modernization and progress, the communists set the fabric of the Afghan society on fire; their belief system and way of life was challenged and attacked. The west, eager to succeed in the Cold War with the Soviets, further factionalized the Afghan society.

Introduction of western way of life in a deeply rooted society of Afghans is either not possible at this time or it might take generations to take root because it is imported and not home grown. Quick impact development projects are like putting a band aid on a deep wound, we are hypothesizing the results. The hearts and minds of the rural Afghan are not going to be won by military actions or by empowering the corrupt, ineffective installed Afghan government and its officials. Asking the rural villagers to assist us in securing their areas from insurgents who are their brothers, kin, or from the same clans by bribing them is not going to work.

No matter what the influential or local power brokers tell us, they all have connections with the insurgents and assist them with donations at all times. Not because their belief system is the same as theirs or they want them to take power, but because of their own survival, just in case we leave and they (the insurgents) are in power again. Introduction of women's rights, human rights, and all other western ideals will take generations for rural areas to adapt.

While the aim of coalition and western powers is to introduce democratic institutions in Afghanistan, like free elections, the people of Afghanistan must choose their own representatives and thus decide their future.

Final Thoughts

Some of the events that have happened recently (late 2011 and early 2012) have a parallel to what I believed needed to happen (as I've written in the preceding pages).

Peace cannot come to Afghanistan unless there is a dialog and compromise with the insurgents:

- For that objective, recently Mullah Omar has been taken off the terrorist group list by the US. The US government has gone so far to say that Mullah Omar is not an enemy of the west.
- The Taliban has been allowed to open an office in Qatar for negotiations to take place.
- The Afghan Taliban who are in Guantanamo would be handed over to Afghan Government.

In addition to Mullah Omar, here are two other important insurgent groups remaining to be dealt with:

Gulbuddin Hekmatyar (the Karzai government has recently been in negotiation with them), the leader of Hizb-e-Islami is a radical Islamist militia that controls territory in Afghanistan's northeast, and was a former ally of the US and the Haqqani group who are still road blocks to peace. And will remain so as long as the Pakistan government perceives them to be beneficial to their national interest. So the Pakistani government has to be brought into the negotiations and be convinced that peace in Afghanistan is not a threat to their national security.

I observed that the coalition forces should not leave Afghanistan and there should be a presence of the allied forces in the country. And that has been decided, and even the Loya Jerga (the national assembly of the Afghans) has approved the long term commitment of the Americans to stay in the country.

But concerns remain:

I still believe that unless a Pashtun is elected as the leader by the Afghans themselves, long term peace is not going to come to the country.

Iran is another emerging player in Afghan peace. With the American and European declaration of further sanctions on Iran; Iran who has relations with the Afghan Government as well as the insurgents will make things tougher for Afghan peace as well as for the western forces. Iran like Pakistan (ordered by Afghanistan and India) does not want two antagonistic forces on its two borders (Iraq and Afghanistan). Although American forces are leaving Iraq, the influence is still there.

So while things are improving there are still a couple of 'doors' that need to be reworked for the Afghan people to step through into a beautiful home of their own—four solid walls, a roof over their heads and the same equality and opportunity that all humans desire and should share in.

ONLY BREATH (by Rumi)
Translated by Coleman Barks

Not Christian or Jew or Muslim, not Hindu,
Buddhist, Sufi, or Zen. Not any religion

or cultural system. I am not from the East
or the West, not out of the ocean or up

from the ground, not natural or ethereal, not
composed of elements at all. I do not exist,

am not an entity in this world or the next,
did not descend from Adam and Eve or any

origin story. My place is placeless, a trace
of the traceless. Neither body nor soul.

I belong to the beloved, have seen the two
worlds as one and that one call to and know,

first, last, outer, inner, only that
breath breathing human being.

www.ingramcontent.com/pod-product-compliance
Lightning Source LLC
Chambersburg PA
CBHW022333280326
41934CB00006B/618